Across an Inland Sea

Across an Inland Sea

WRITING IN PLACE FROM
BUFFALO TO BERLIN

Nicholas Howe

PRINCETON UNIVERSITY PRESS

PRINCETON AND OXFORD

Library of Congress Cataloging-in-Publication Data

Howe, Nicholas.
Across an inland sea : writing in place from Buffalo to Berlin / Nicholas Howe.
p. cm.
Includes bibliographical references.
ISBN 0-691-11365-3 (acid-free paper)
1. Howe, Nicholas—homes and haunts. 2. English teachers—United States—
Biography. 3. College teachers—United States—Biography. 4. Medievalists—
United States—Biography. 5. Anglicists—United States—Biography.
6. Americans—Europe—Biography. 7. Place (Philosophy) 8. Authorship. I. Title.
PE64.H69 A3 2003
820.9—dc21
[B]   2002031744

British Library Cataloging-in-Publication Data available.

This book has been composed in Goudy

Printed on acid-free paper.∞

www.pupress.princeton.edu

Printed in the United States of America

10 9 8 7 6 5 4 3 2 1

For Georgina

I pity the man who can travel from *Dan* to *Beersheba*, and cry, 'Tis all barren—and so it is; and so is all the world to him who will not cultivate the fruits it offers.

—Laurence Sterne, *Sentimental Journey*

The places we have known do not belong only to the world of space on which we map them for our own convenience. None of them was ever more than a thin slice, held between the contiguous impressions that composed our life at that time; the memory of a particular image is but regret for a particular moment; and houses, roads, avenues are as fugitive, alas, as the years.

—Marcel Proust, *Swann's Way*

Contents

Across an Inland Sea

Inland Sea: Buffalo and Beyond

At the start of the twentieth century, my mother's parents left Greece to settle in Buffalo, New York. Earlier in the Greek diaspora, they would have gone to another inland port, to Trebizond on the Black Sea or, most likely, to Alexandria on the Mediterranean. There were distant cousins on my grandmother's side who had settled there; as a young girl my mother met them in Athens where the family had gathered for a reunion in 1928. I sometimes wonder if these cousins knew of Cavafy when he lived in Alexandria and wrote his poems about coming home to Ithaca or waiting for barbarians at the end of things. I have no way of knowing, though, because we lost all trace of them long ago. They would not have been likely to approve of Cavafy; he was a poet, homosexual, anglophile, in short, an alienated native of the Levant rather than a loyal son of Hellas. And family gossip said that our cousins were provincial in ways that only those who live in the ruins of a great civilization can be, for they could always find in the past what they lacked in the present.

CHAPTER 1

Had my grandfather settled in Trebizond or Alexandria, this book about places persisting in memory might have been easier to write because those cities have the dusty glamour of old trade routes. But it was Buffalo where he settled, and brought my grandmother after they married, and thus I cannot trade on the romance of lost empire. Instead, I write about Buffalo from the late 1950s through the early 1990s when no travel writer would have put it on his trophy list. It might have earned a brief mention in an itinerary for Niagara Falls, and in that way perhaps have repeated my grandfather's experience. For a few years as a young man he drove a sightseeing bus from the Buffalo train station to the Falls. It was quick tourism before World War I: jump off a New York Central, see a wonder of the world, catch another train out.

Thirty-five years are a brief span in the life of a city but those from the late 1950s through the early 1990s marked a change in Buffalo. When I was growing up the Chamber of Commerce proclaimed "Boost Buffalo. It's good for you." As recently as the late seventies you could see these words on the sides of buildings, though the paint had faded and the offices inside were sometimes unoccupied. By then the city was learning to take pride in a more hard-boiled slogan, "Buffalo. City of No Illusions." Being a city of no illusions meant having a kind of weary dignity, a toughness that came from a large working-class population, bad winters, and a suspicion about more cosmopolitan parts of the state, especially New York City. Buffalo knew what it meant to be a city of casualty, a place that *Sports Illustrated* once called "The Armpit of the East." The journalist, as usual, got it wrong because Buffalo is not really a city of the eastern United States. It began to thrive only after it became the western terminus for the Erie Canal in the late 1820s. To

2

this day, it still feels more than superficially midwestern in its attitudes and tastes.

The city has this feel because, resting on the eastern edge of Lake Erie, it belongs to the inland waterways that give coherence to the center of the continent. Starting from Buffalo, you move west to Erie, Cleveland, Toledo, Detroit, Chicago, Milwaukee, Duluth. Along that network of lakes and rivers runs as well a shared cultural identity, for many who settled in these Rust Belt cities were immigrants in the 1840s and 1850s from Germany and then, in later decades, from Poland and elsewhere in Eastern Europe. Like other cities on the great midwestern lakes, Buffalo once took pride in its local beers: Simon Pure, Kochs, Iroquois, to name only three I drank as a teenager. They were cheaper than the national brands and certainly tasted no worse. Their neon signs dotted the small windows of the corner taverns that could be found in the city's older neighborhoods. Now that these breweries have gone out of business, the city has lost some of its flavor. The new microbreweries make better beer, but they are too decorous to splash their names in blue and red neon across the local bars where people gather after work or eat a fishfry on Friday evening.

From where I write in Columbus, it is six hours on the interstate to Buffalo: two hours northeast through Ohio, and the rest along the rim of Lake Erie past the outskirts of Cleveland through Pennsylvania and then into New York State. For this part of the trip you drive within a few miles of the lake. On the interstate, especially in Pennsylvania as it approaches New York, you ride high on the old escarpment and for a few miles look down, across acres of vineyard, to the hard blueness of the lake. For most of these four hours you cannot see the lake, though if you drive the route regularly you learn to feel its almost oceanic presence because rain showers and snow squalls can blow off it with remark-able ferocity. More immediately, you realize after crossing the state line into New York that you are riding on what had once been the bed of the lake before it shrank to its current size. Driving that route, I came to feel the persis-tence of geography in life, especially as it gives form to mem-ory. From those hours of driving toward Buffalo I learned how much that somber city had left its impress on me in ways that more inviting or glamourous places have never done and never will.

The somberness of the city had everything to do with its structures: huge factories to roll steel, tower after tower of elevators to store grain, lift bridges to give lakeboats access along the Buffalo River. The great buildings of its downtown date from a time when elegance, even modernity, meant a heavy solemnity, a lavish use of stone and tile to hide iron-work skeletons. These structures were put there to endure, and today some survive sadly without purpose. They stand against the lake and its hard weather with a kind of reassur-ance that more minimal buildings from late in the twentieth century cannot offer. Their heavy construction makes these turn-of-the-century buildings a nightmare for wreckers. So many of them remain because sometimes the best way to destroy is to abandon.

In winter when dusk comes early, there is never enough light in Buffalo. It has the heavy clouds typical of a city on the water. Summers in Buffalo are usually cool and sunny, but they have nothing to do with shaping the character of the place. It is the long soul-wearying grayness from late October through early April that defines the city. The snow does so as well, of course, but it falls unevenly over western New York. Towns a few miles to the south of Buffalo can dig out from two feet of snow while towns the same distance to the north sweep away a light dusting. In the American imagination, Buffalo remains a snow capital because during one winter in each generation it suffers a massive storm that takes weeks to clear away. In flood regions, people point with pride to the high-water line on bridges or buildings; in Buffalo, they do the same with drifts that buried houses and filled underpasses.

It is the slag-gray clouds that weigh down on you for months and exhaust you during Buffalo winters. The sun when it appears seems watery and distant behind a thin glaze of cloud. In the older sections of the city, the houses are narrow and tall, typically two full stories and a usable attic. They were built close together with barely enough space between them for a single car to reach the garages in back. In these older neighborhoods, whether modest working-class or solidly upper-middle-class, the city has a cramped feel about it that has nothing to do with the constraints of topography. Only on the west side, with the lake and river, do natural boundaries press the city in on itself. No, the older houses in Buffalo cluster together to stand against the wind that blows, unbroken, across the lake from Canada. And the rooms in these houses, with their high windows and heavy woodwork, are dark. The houses have a quality of old-fashioned propriety in their darkness, of domestic life as the defining source of one's being.

In a city like Buffalo, life did not move into a public world except for church and tavern, and both are also defining and limiting in their sense of community. In the old areas, where no false piety separated church and tavern, neighborhood locals could be found on many street corners. They were usually quiet, clean, orderly. Dark booths and a few tables, a bar with blended whiskies and local draft beers, a small menu with beef on weck (the local hardroll dotted with rock salt and caraway seeds) and a vinegar-laced German potato salad—these were places where families would come for a little cheer against the winter gloom. By no accident, one of the few good books about Buffalo, Verlyn Klinkenborg's *The Last Fine Time*, is set in a tavern called "George & Eddie's," a place as unassuming as its name. Or, that once was as unassuming as its name; it's gone now as is most of the old east-side Polish community where it was located. The Eddie of George & Eddie's lived about half a mile from where I grew up in the suburbs, another one of those who left the old neighborhood for the comforts of a new house with a green backyard.

The artist who knew how to paint those grim Buffalo neighborhoods was Charles Burchfield, whose scenes of tall, narrow houses and wind-tormented trees have for Buffalonians an almost photographic realism. With their eerie vibrations, his paintings seem hallucinogenic only to those who have never spent a winter in Buffalo. His houses shimmer weirdly along their edges; verticals we know to be plumb and foursquare waver; houses and streets are set at disconcerting angles that make for a feeling of dislocation. His trees are more gnarled than any you can find in nature, their branches form haloes of light that give a feeling of unease. If Burchfield and Edward Hopper are often paired as American realists, their subjects are different. Hopper captures those moments when people seem overwhelmed by the emptiness of the cityscape. Burchfield paints the psychic disturbance one senses in the city itself; his buildings vibrate with the unseen, unexpressed emotions of those who live within them. Looking at his scenes of Buffalo, at such paintings as *Ice Glare* or *Sulphurous Evening*, one feels the waves of repression that emanate from his houses. These are not places where happy people live. They are the houses of those who maintain outward appearances and who know that things inside have gotten terribly twisted.

This spookiness fills the houses in his famous *Promenade*, but to see it you have to look past the episode he paints on the sidewalk of a fat woman with a little dog being followed by a pack of big dogs. The painting seems comic, but turns ominous because the houses in the scene refuse to be merely picturesque. The elegiac Burchfield is less, however, the painter of city neighborhoods or backyards filled with massive trees than the recorder of urban industry in works with austere titles like *Ice-Bound Lake Boats*, *Freight Cars Under a Bridge*, or *Black Iron*, a meticulous rendering of a railroad lift bridge on a heavy overcast day in fall. In a work of 1929, Burchfield seems to predict the fate of industrial Buffalo by painting a pile of old boilers, gearworks, and pipes as *Still Life—Scrap Iron*. Burchfield's industrial paintings seem elegiac because of all that happened to the city since he did them: its decline, its loss of a center, its hard years of layoffs and canceled dreams. Or perhaps that decline is why I look at his paintings with the conviction that through some detail they might teach me to understand why the city changed so fundamentally.

The city's original reason for being, its place on the map, came from the confluence of the Buffalo River into the Niagara River as it flowed from Lake Erie to Lake Ontario. Travel by water turned Buffalo into the eastern edge of the American midwest. The neighborhood near Buffalo Harbor remembers the regions on the far side of the lake and beyond with streets named Ohio, Indiana, Illinois, Michigan, Mississippi. As an inland port, Buffalo lost its being after the St. Lawrence Seaway opened in the late 1950s. Once ocean-going freighters could move through the Great Lakes to unload their cargoes and then reload with grain or ore, Buffalo no longer served as a center for transshipment between lake-boats and freightcars. The trainyards that sprawl across the southern parts of Buffalo belong to a lost city. But once, in the war year of 1943 when food was as vital as munitions, Buffalo shipped more grain in a single year than any other harbor ever did in history. The city, as family stories told, had not always been a backwater.

During the 1960s and early 1970s, Buffalo became a monument to the passing of the high-industrial age. Its mills and elevators remained intact but lost much of their utility and seemed to offer no possibilities for reuse. For a time the city had known scale, energy, sweat. It had been a place of transformation where grain was milled into flour and breakfast cereal, where iron ore and coke were smelted to steel for carframes and bridge girders. It was a city that knew the basic elements of life, that dealt in the changes worked by fire and water. So how had it been left to die? How had it become a monument to ways of living that no one cared about anymore?

These questions came too late, after those I might have asked had died. There were some answers that did not require family knowledge. Buffalo was part of the decline of the industrial heartland into Rust Belt; it was hit like other cities on this inland sea by rises in energy prices, labor costs, and racial unrest; it was, more uniquely, made anachronistic by changes in transportation patterns. These are all necessary explanations and others might be added. But none help me to discover what it was like to have lived through this decline. What did it mean to feel the city's life drift elsewhere, to know almost imperceptibly over time the withering of a city's identity? What did it mean to grow old in that city as it also aged and slipped into memory?

My ghosts of Buffalo come from the city's majesty before the 1950s. I want to recover that city and find my family's time in it; I want place to be a means to locate what has been lost in our lives. In classical Greek, the rhetorical patterns in stories are called *topoi* and are related etymologically to *topography*: these patterns provide the terrain of stories. In turn, stories can be a way of mapping the geography of a place. Memory is the quality of place that explains its hold on us; observation must be another because it can reveal the deceptions of memory. What holds them together is the shared meaning of stories: those we bring to a place and those we create about it. And most of our stories about place have more or less to do with the treacheries of time.

The stories of place that I heard as a child were complicated further by being always about two places at the same moment. Nothing my grandparents told me about their early years in Buffalo was just about Buffalo. Their stories were immigrants' stories, and they held Greece in their imagination as well. Stories were about times and places; they were told to make sense of the rent in their experience between their lives in an American city and their past in villages of the Peloponnesus. Unlike immigrants from other parts of Europe, my grandparents were able to visit Greece regularly. With that movement back and forth came a renewal of stories, a deeper sense that connections between places were never set in fixed form but were always fluid. Living as they did, they could never have a single sense of place but instead told their stories from shifting perspectives and moments.

In the late 1970s, I would go home to Buffalo from New York City by train. The line was Amtrak, not the New York Central, but the route was the same as it had been for generations because it followed the lay of the land. Running straight north from the city on the eastern bank of the Hudson you would gaze for two hours or so at nineteenth-century bracketed houses in the near foreground and at the Catskills in the distance across the river. At certain moments, sometimes even for long stretches, the view from the train was as it would have been in the 1870s because nothing of our time was visible. Then suddenly there would be huge gravel pits and cement factories scarring the far bank, nuclear power plants, diesel tugs with strings of river barges, the occasional powerboat breaking a crest. At Albany, as the train crossed the river, you caught a glimpse of the state capitol, and then began the most haunted stage of the trip through the Mohawk River Valley, past old towns like Amsterdam and Herkimer with three-story brick factories and hulking water towers. In the valley, the train ran parallel to the remains of the Erie Canal, past cut-stone locks built foursquare into hillsides and modest houses for lockkeepers. By Syracuse, the landscape gave out to flat stretches but in winter, as I was going home for Christmas, the change hardly mattered because by then it would have grown dark in the heavy, closed-down way it gets dark in upstate New York. For the last two hours the train would run west to Buffalo through one-street villages where at night all you could see was a level-grade crossing and a tavern with neon signs for Genesee beer.

That run through New York State was a long and gentle way to reenter home; it gave me hours to read and smoke, to close for a time the ever-widening distance that seemed to be growing between my life in New York and my past in Buffalo. I didn't then have the strength to make the trip home by plane in an hour; there was too much to think through and clear away. I would often dream during that trip about my grandfather riding the train in the 1920s after his law practice grew beyond the confines of Buffalo, or of my mother taking it in the 1940s when she left for graduate school at Columbia. For much of the trip, especially in the winter evening, there was nothing visible that would not have been there for them to have seen decades before. To go home to Buffalo as they had gone home seemed a way to connect with them. A drink or two in the bar car would help, especially because on the last stage of the trip after Rochester there were very few people aboard. It was quiet and one could think. At such moments, I tried to write a short story in my head about a man who loved that terrain, who knew it was the blood of his life. All that made him exceptional was his knowledge that he was linked to the soil and sky of western New York. I never wrote the story; it was no more than a mood one might have looking out a train window. It would have been called "The Landscape Artist."

Coming into Buffalo, the red-white-and-blue Amtrak train would pass through the old yards left over from the city's days as a center of transshipment, when it was second only to Chicago in its rail capacity. At the edge of those yards, standing alone, was the passenger station; located in the residential east side on Paderewski Drive, it was surprisingly far from downtown. This imperial edifice, to use a necessarily pompous phrase, was built in 1929. Its twenty-story office tower in Art Deco style was meant to balance the city hall some three miles away across the skyline. The station seemed grander for being in the midst of the modest frame houses and parish churches of the old Polish neighborhood. Now, that station tower looms over the city like an obelisk commemorating some victory in a long-forgotten war. It remains, but nobody quite knows why it was built in the first place. The station, as the stories agree, had been set far from

11

downtown at the demand of the New York Central, which did not want its express trains between New York and Chicago delayed by entry into the heart of Buffalo. At the edge of the city, the station could receive the Twentieth-Century Limited for a moment before it would head south along the escarpment of Lake Erie or east across the fields of upstate New York. The city's place was calibrated precisely: it rated a stop by the fastest trains, but only for a moment, and only on its periphery.

By the late seventies, three or four Amtrak trains a day would move through the station. That they stopped on the edge of the city seemed absurd because the fast trains had been gone for generations. No one taking a train to Buffalo in the 1970s was worried about speed. The passengers had time to kill or needed that time to get ready for coming home. Once off the train in Buffalo, you walked up the stairs from the platform to a walkway that led into the great waiting room of the station. There under a soaring Italianate vaulted ceiling of tile stood bank after bank of oak benches set back to back. They filled the room and could hold hundreds of people. They were empty now, dusty and dull because no one sat on them and polished their wood to a warm glow. Beyond the waiting room was a grand concourse that once held shops of all sorts: jeweler, clothier, florist, restaurant. They were gone, leaving behind only their signs. A newsstand and a small lunch counter for coffee and hot dogs were still open. All that ran through the space were the echoing sounds of passengers crowding the front curb where family and friends were waiting in cars.

In its emptiness, this space had the beauty of heartache. It should have been swarming with noise and motion, with people as jazzed as the great express trains that once waited below, impatient to head off at speed. The building was intact but a ruin—its time had passed and there was nothing to do with it so far from downtown. Waiting for me at the end of my trip, perched on one of the oak benches as she had years before in her youth, was my mother. The first few times she met me there she would tell her stories about taking the train from New York during World War II when, a beautiful young woman, she was surrounded by GIs on the move. She would always say that in those years the waiting room was so full that people sat on the floor and lined up by the dozens to get a sandwich and coffee. And then she would talk about the building, pointing especially to the details of its vaulted ceiling, and appreciating them with her art-historian's eye. I know now that she gave these impromptu lectures to distract herself from the pain she felt at seeing this building in her beloved city standing on the edge of abandonment.

My mother came back to Buffalo after a divorce in the early 1960s because she wanted to give us the protection of her family, and that protection was tied in subtle, unbroken ways to the solace of place. Whatever happened, she seemed to think, my sister and I would grow up safely if we were living in her city. Now, almost ten years after her death, I can only think of her in Buffalo. Placing her there, I understand her romantic character, her particular mixture of will and melancholy. She had wanted as a young woman to leave for the big city, like the hero of a nineteenth-century novel, and went to New York to get her Ph.D. at Columbia in Classics and Archaeology under émigré German scholars. That decision meant disappointing her father, who above all wanted her to marry a well-connected Greek-American, perhaps a son of one of his fellow immigrants who had made good. She married instead a poor Jewish socialist, a man who was in all ways unimaginable to her father. Both my parents

13

were children of immigrants, both knew their parents' stories of dislocation. In ways neither ever expressed to me, that must have been part of their life together. The years of their marriage, spent first in New York and then in Boston, now seem to me an interlude in her life, a respite from the hold Buffalo held over her. Through some destiny her character made for her, she had to go home to that city, to live among the same streets and walk along the river she had known as a girl. That eased the pain of dislocation for her.

The last time I took the train to Buffalo, I waited at the station for my mother for more than half an hour. Worried by her absence—she who was always punctual—I could not conceive of why she was not there. And then she did come, agitated and a bit disoriented. She had heard that Amtrak was closing the old station and opening a new one near her house in the suburbs. So she had gone there to meet me but found it was only a construction site where she had almost gotten her car stuck in the mud. She was caught painfully between two maps of the city: one that she knew from her youth and one that was being redrafted by the city's sprawl. We both knew then there would be no reason for me to take the train to Buffalo when it meant getting off at a prefab metal building far from downtown.

The old station on Paderewski Drive had a large bronze statue of a buffalo that greeted passengers on their entry. It was a wonderfully literal sign of place, one that went with the character of the city: straightforward, unornamented, a bit slow but capable of great power when needed. In his story "I am Dying, Egypt, Dying," John Updike has a character remember this statue as he, far from his home in Buffalo, suffers a middle-aged encounter with despair on a tourist boat on the Nile. From one monument of place to another, Updike seems to imply, we measure out the crises in our lives.

In a memory I alone seem to have, this statue of a buffalo was displayed in the main terminal of the Buffalo International Airport where it greeted passengers of a later era. I have since looked for the statue there but have not found it. Friends tell me they do not remember that it was ever in the airport, though a replica of the original was recently placed on the suburban campus of the University at Buffalo. In a fragmented city, that may well be the only public space where anyone can come and go. But that buffalo no longer greets anyone entering the city as a sign of the place.

Of the hundreds of family photographs I inherited after my mother's death, one has held me with a steady fascination. This photograph—a black and white kodak "snap," undated, its surface emulsion cracked—shows my grandmother Urania Phillies standing outside the house in Buffalo where the family lived for over forty years and where my mother Thalia grew up. The season is winter, with a barely cleared street and sidewalk visible, and perhaps two feet of snow on the ground. The powerful elms along the sidewalks are bare but enough of their branches are visible to show they would arch the streets with shade in spring and summer. My grandmother wears a dark coat and hat, her hands are folded across her front, she looks straight at the camera perhaps twenty feet away. Her feet are hidden by a small mound of snow but she must be wearing arctics. She smiles and holds herself with the posture of a well-bred woman who grew up in another country late in the nineteenth century. Behind her, on the far side of the cross street, a man stands with his right foot off the ground as if to shake snow from his galoshes. Like my grandmother, this stranger wears the clothes that prevail in cold places for generations, unchanged by fashion.

15

There are no cars visible in the photo. The houses were built perhaps thirty years before my grandparents moved to the corner of Hodge and Ashland in 1917. There is nothing in the scene to date the photo. My grandmother's face is visible but with insufficient detail to help me calculate her age. And, like other women in the family, she had the gift of seeming younger than she was. I would guess it's the late twenties, perhaps the early thirties. On the back of the photo, my aunt Katherine has written in English, "This is mama." And then, in a beautifully clear hand, has added in a Greek that a friend translated for me: "Do you remember when we took it? This is how much snow we have now. Tonight it is snowing a lot." That message suggests the photo was meant for a relative or family friend who had visited Buffalo earlier that winter. And then, for some reason, it was never mailed.

There is nothing remarkable about the photo. I stare at it, though, because it sets my grandmother in the city where she lived for more than sixty years. What it shows might have been any winter over those years, any number of just-fallen snows. There is no story here, not even a memorable moment or episode that might in family tradition have become a story. There is only a woman standing on the sidewalk next to her house, as she did every winter until she and her husband moved to the suburbs around 1950. What endures for me in this photograph is the presence of place, the reminder that my grandmother spent much of her life in that narrow gray house at the corner of Hodge and Ashland. It matters as well that she and my grandfather left that house before I was born, though it remained their property until they both died in 1971. I remember being in it only once, when my mother and I cleaned out the attic before putting it up for sale. There was not much left, only a few bound volumes of *National Geographic* and some odd bits and pieces of clothing. It took very little time to gather what was left into the trash.

This house still holds most of the family stories I know. The elm trees along Ashland and Hodge are long gone to disease but otherwise the scene would look much the same now in winter as it did seventy years ago when my grand-mother posed for the camera. To this day, you can see the initials "EP" my uncle Eustace Phillies carved into the brick of the building next door. The neighborhood went down a bit in the 1960s but now has come back to the comfortable solidity it knew years ago. When I would visit my mother in Buffalo and we would find ourselves downtown on family business at the lawyer's office or bank, we would drive by the house on Hodge Avenue to see how it looked. No longer ours, it remained in the family by the right of prior occupancy.

I visited the house on Hodge Avenue two days after my mother died in 1993. She lived then far from downtown Buffalo in a suburb beyond the new university campus. That was no place to grieve for her, no place to hold the duration of her life. So we went, my sister and I and a few others in our early forties, to eat dinner and talk about her in a restaurant around the corner from where she had grown up. When she lived on Hodge Avenue, the building had been a German delicatessen where the family bought cold cuts and potato salad for Sunday night supper. Now it was an elegantly minimalist Italian restaurant with the improbable name of "BFLO Rome."

For the space of that dinner, the three generations of the family—almost a century's worth by then—could be held together in memory by stories because for one last time those who remained were set in a common place. But the fact is, the stories had begun to disappear long before that evening, once those of my generation left Buffalo to live elsewhere. For one can carry away only so many stories of home before they take on the sour taste of nostalgia. Nor does telling them to strangers revive the stories. It can only preserve them, as in a memoir, and preservation is not my interest. Rather, thinking about these family stories allows me to think about their setting, the sense of place that enfolds them and survives at least in part their disappearance.

The endurance of place haunts all the stories I remember about Buffalo. All of the ways I write about places in this book begin in the stories I grew up hearing about this city on the eastern shore of an inland sea. Buffalo, Queen City of the Great Lakes. The title has an old fashioned sound to it that suggests fixed ways. Cities are female because, like Rome, they must be maternal; and the lakes are great because, like everything else in nineteenth-century America, their scale demanded excess. Now, when other cities call themselves "world-class" or "cosmopolitan" or "multicultural," there is a faded and honorably provincial tone to this forgotten title for Buffalo.

This faded tone is the only true one for writing about the Buffalo I remember. Growing up there taught me an affection for cities and places that had been left behind. Or, more exactly, for those corners in cities that seemed to hold almost intact the ways of earlier generations. There was a sense as you traveled through neighborhoods in Buffalo that you were moving across different decades because each section retained the time of its construction. This sense that different eras were fossilized each in its own area of the city had much to do with Buffalo's lack of economic prosperity. Not unhappily it also meant that such masterpieces as Louis Sullivan's Prudential Building or D.H. Burnham's Ellicott

Square Building, both dating from 1895–96, were never torn down in some benighted campaign of urban renewal. There was never the need or the means to rebuild downtown Buffalo in a systematic way. A few old buildings were torn down, some new structures went up, almost all of them for banking or government, but they did not threaten the older ones around them. There simply was never enough money in Buffalo for that to happen. They showed the workings of time, those faded monumental buildings from the 1890s, and they colored the way you learned to look at everything around them.

As she had asked, we scattered my mother's remains into the Niagara River as it flows north from the city of Buffalo toward Niagara Falls. There, standing on a breakwater she had walked since her childhood, my sister and I along with our spouses tossed handfuls of gritty ash and bone into the river. It was a walk she loved because there the river ran dangerously fast and deep, and seemed for her the place where in her inland life she could dream most vividly of elsewhere. In the years before she died, she took to going back to the breakwater where she would walk and remember a city that she had known in the 1920s and 1930s but that had changed almost beyond her ability to recognize and accept. The walk along the breakwater remained, but the inland port downriver was passing. Many of the grain elevators were empty and the steel mills south of the city no longer burned red through the night.

Stubbornly, my mother kept her safe-deposit box in a grand, beautifully-domed bank, far from where she lived, so that she would have some reason to go downtown from time to time. The box had been her mother's before her, and in the last years of her life it was listed under my name and my

19

sister's. When the time came to empty it, to close out the family's connection with that bank, and the city as well, there was very little to take away. Some insurance policies, a list of serial numbers, a few pieces of unworn jewelry. For thirty years and more there had been no reason to keep a safe-deposit box in that bank, except of course for the only one that mattered to my mother. Each time she went there she quietly visited with the ghosts of her city. That was the treasure she most cherished in her romantic soul and, in ways I only understand as I write these sentences, the richest inheritance she could leave to me. For part of each visit I made back to Buffalo as she grew older was to go to that safe-deposit box to add or remove papers as needed. The errand was her way to guide me through the city she had known when she was growing up and to which she returned in her forties with my sister and me.

Working my way back to stories from my childhood in Buffalo, I realize that most have slipped away as old stories usually do. But the process is not simply one of forgetting. Some were no more than a flash in memory: my mother reminiscing about lying in bed on a summer night and hearing the sound of gunfire on the Niagara River as Treasury agents chased rumrunners crossing over from Fort Erie, Ontario, during Prohibition. Other of these stories would take a lifetime of archaeology to reconstruct: my grandfather discoursing on the ways in which as an attorney he was free to practice within the Greek community, but met great prejudice from the legal establishment when he became the best industrial negligence lawyer in the city. That was a busy practice, for Buffalo was full of dangerous mills and factories, and with badly trained immigrant workers who had been given the dirty jobs to do. He sued on behalf of maimed and burned workers, slipping into the accents of an immigrant's English when pleading to a jury of fellow immigrants, and he felt a sense of the newcomer's triumph when he forced the insurance companies to settle cases. He knew enough about the dynamics of class in America to keep his offices in the best building in Buffalo: he loved having the top-floor corner of the Ellicott Square Building with its view of Lake Erie. Every morning he stopped in the florist's shop in the lobby for his boutonniere. Elegance mattered for a lawyer who made his living in a working-class city by suing corporations.

I resist going further because I know that soon I will move from remembering to inventing. As he meditated on accounts he had read of Atlantis, Montaigne said, "We need topographers to give us exact descriptions of the places where they have been." Such topographers should speak only of what they know directly. His caution seems especially necessary when writing about lost continents that have faded to the edges of memory. Most of my Buffalo stories have faded in that way because I never knew the city where they were set. Most of the city that mattered in the telling of these family stories was in one way or another off-limits to me: the ghetto that burned in the race riots of 1967, and also the white working-class neighborhoods of Black Rock and South Buffalo, as well as the few surviving enclaves of WASP privilege in quiet streets off Delaware Park. My Buffalo was that of a suburban child, one distanced from the city but without a center of his own.

We went downtown to Memorial Auditorium to watch the local Catholic colleges—Canisius, St. Bonaventure, Niagara—play basketball, or to War Memorial Stadium to see the Bisons play AAA baseball when the International League lived up to its name. The "Rockpile," as this stadium was known, is gone now but it survived long enough to be the setting for 1920s baseball as depicted in the film version of *The Natural*. Even as a kid I knew those places were old and shabby, but that was part of their charm. They were memorials for things past, as their names said, and they did not heed the suburban imperative that made easy parking the important thing in life. These were places where tough, undertalented athletes tried to make it. They rarely did, but the city loved them all the more for their slowness or their lack of grace. All it asked was that they play hurt and bleeding, that they remember they were lucky not to be working graveyard at Bethlehem Steel or Hooker Chemical.

We also went downtown to Kleinhans Music Hall for the Tuesday night chamber music series when the Budapest String Quartet played, or to the Albright-Knox Art Gallery for its collection of late-nineteenth– and twentieth-century art. It became something of a family joke to take out-of-town visitors to the gallery where they expected to see a few minor pieces by overrated artists that the provincials wanted to show off as masterpieces. When they saw instead a long wall of paintings familiar to them from textbooks—Gauguin's *Yellow Christ* and *Spirit of the Dead Watching*, to name only two—they would mumble apologies about their mistaken expectations. At such moments, I learned what it meant to be growing up in a city that outsiders would call, in a gesture of politeness, provincial.

The collection of that gallery is one of the most durable memories I have of Buffalo as a place. I spent many hours there with my mother and her students as they worked their way from the early Impressionists to the latest Op Art. Now, years later, when I go to a show of a major twentieth-century artist I expect sooner or later to find a work I know from Buffalo. That collection has become for me a movable feast of the place, one that stands for the complexity of the city. It matters as well where I see this piece on loan from Buffalo displayed—in New York or Paris or some other world-class city—for that experience of dislocation enriches my memories of having lived on an inland sea.

For all that I grew up in Buffalo hearing its stories, I did not live in the place of those stories; the connections between the stories and the place were drawn very thin by time. Growing up in a place means that you know it and yet don't, that your knowledge of the place means an intimacy with scene, landscape, people, and also an ignorance of scene, landscape, people. The native's knowledge is partial and biased in ways that the scholar's, for example, should not be. It affects my sense of Buffalo that I am ignorant about certain neighborhoods and certain stories. It alters my sense of the place that I know about the community of working-class lesbians who lived in Buffalo through the 1950s only because Elizabeth Lapovsky Kennedy and Madeline D. Davis published a fine book in 1993 called *Boots of Leather, Slippers of Gold*. Yet this book is so true to the larger place where these women lived that it also becomes a book about Buffalo as a city.

It also matters to this chronicle that my sense of Buffalo is frozen in a set time—like a slice of tissue prepared for biopsy—from the late 1950s to 1993, when my mother died and my vital connection to the place lapsed. That time in Buffalo is the most immutable experience of my life but it was brief: from the age of eleven to seventeen, from sixth grade until my departure for college in Toronto. The city shaped me with its stubborn, unshiftable gravity: the place had weight. Perhaps it was dying of its own weight in the American landscape but there was nothing flimsy or wind-blown about it. The city was already in its decline in those

23

years from 1964 to 1970, though its grayest time was yet to come. Still, it was populated by those who had grown up and thrived in the years when it was the capital port on the great inland sea of North America.

Of the port of Buffalo, I remember best the twice-yearly stories on the local TV news about the last ship to leave in the fall before ice closed the harbor and the first to arrive in spring after icebreakers opened the way. There would be an occasional story of some forlorn freighter from Taiwan or Panama that got iced in because it had waited too long to leave. Its crew, or at least some of them, would spend a lonely winter in Buffalo keeping their ship safe and growing crazy from boredom. The local community feeding them dinner at Christmas always made a good human-interest story in the Buffalo *Evening News* or *Courier Express*.

During the 1960s Lake Erie was dying a slow death from the waste that washed into it from the American heartland. I knew the lake was sick precisely because I could not know it as my mother and her generation had known it. We did not take the lakeboat *Canadiana* to the amusement park at Crystal Beach, nor did we swim off Windmill Point in Ontario. And we certainly did not eat the whitefish that had been a Friday night staple across Catholic Buffalo for decades. In the late twentieth century, inland seas are fated to become holding tanks for run-off from the surrounding regions: river silt, excess fertilizer, discharged sewage, chemical pollution, family stories. In his brilliant *Black Sea*, Neal Ascherson describes a body of water dying from the bottom up as it loses the oxygen necessary for survival. These inland seas and their great trading cities have in our time reverted to backwaters where things slip away into obscurity. The Black Sea fleet of the Soviet Union rusts in the dockyards of Odessa, just as a few forlorn naval vessels are anchored in Buffalo Harbor as a tourist attraction. These seagoing vessels of World War II vintage reached Buffalo through the opening of the St. Lawrence Seaway. They seem a sad return to the city for the opening of its harbor to the high seas.

There was very little rooted or sustaining about Buffalo as a place during my years there because I saw the city changing around my mother in ways that she could recognize but never fully absorb. The betrayal of place is that we ask it to remain constant and yet it too must change utterly. The continuity that she knew in Buffalo then was more and more a continuity of shadows: buildings remembered that no longer existed, the dead as they walked the streets where memory found them, the lake as it grew foul and polluted. Cities on inland seas are places where life lingers on too long in the old ways.

Writing about Buffalo becomes a way to see the subject of place through the filter of family memory: it becomes a way to consider place as a measure of broken continuity as generations pass and die off, but also as the site itself changes. Places, if they are to counter the betrayals of time, should have a reassuring solidity to them. We speak of things being set in place, of things fixed, rooted, connected. To think about place should be easier than to think about time because the first can be located in palpable ways, while the second is present only through the indirection of measurement. Stories, family sayings, chronicles: such are the ways time registers in place.

There are questions about place that travel writers cannot ask because they work by passing through in search of the immediate and colorful. They need to find vivid or memorable anecdotes to keep drowsy readers awake. They rarely remain behind to write chronicles of decline. Perhaps it is all forms of chronicle, all narratives of human beings set in place over time, that elude travel writers. Their accounts are about movement, curiosity, change. These writers have always one great advantage: when life becomes unpleasant or boring, they can move on to somewhere else. Alert readers always know that the travel writer has already moved on, to that place where the book in their hands was written. An account of living in a place cannot have this same escape; its writer is always returning, trying to find a way back to the place known earlier in life, and left behind for other sites.

This search for the "heart's field," to use Eudora Welty's phrase for the desired place, has nothing at all to do with the old cliché that you can't go home again. American life and American books are in fact condemned to that particular story. No, it is that one never does finally leave home. Years can pass spent in different sites, one's being shifts along the gravity of time; but some memory, if only a faint smear, remains of where one first knew what it might mean to have a sense of place, even a deep attachment to place. Sometimes the writer's return to where memory took its setting can seem an act of obliteration, an attempt to level what remains, to plow it under and then to salt the earth. These accounts of place, often written from a far distance, begin in loathing yet often end in elegy. Think of James Joyce in *Ulysses* remembering Dublin from Trieste, another inland port that fell on hard times.

The last birthday present my mother gave me was two images of Buffalo: an undated nineteenth-century engraving of the Erie Canal Basin with a grain elevator in the background and an old man fishing in the foreground; and a cover from the July 1951 issue of *Fortune* showing a montage of grain elevators and lakeboats above the title "Made in

Buffalo." Perhaps seventy-five years separate these two images but they tell the same story about the city and its
sources of wealth and power, a story I came too late to see
for myself. Reading that *Fortune* article in the microfilm
room of my library, I discovered it was twelve pages of slick
industrial photography celebrating Buffalo as a shrine to the
myth of the machine. The boys at the Buffalo Chamber of
Commerce must have loved the article when it appeared,
for it boosted the city for every businessman in America to
see. And, for reasons they—or, more likely, their children—
would come to regret, readers in Buffalo probably believed
every word of it in 1951.

The images in the article were by then the clichés of the
genre: photos that showed industrial power with huge machines and few workers. The text carries conviction even
today because it begins with the facts of geography: "Within
500 miles [of Buffalo] are located seven of the eight biggest
U.S. market cities, nearly half the U.S. population, 70 per
cent of Canada's." The geography is 1951, before America's
market cities moved west and south. So too the article's
politics date from that time: "Predominantly Catholic, Buffalo labor is probably the most highly organized in the U.S.
It is also anti-Red and often votes Republican." Turning the
pages and identifying the corporations pictured in these
photos was like taking a drive through the industrial cityscape of my childhood: the grain companies, Bethlehem
Steel, American Brass, Wurlitzer, American Machine and
Foundry, Buffalo Forge, Chevrolet, Harrison Radiator, West-
inghouse, and a few specialty craft firms like Kittinger Furniture and Birge Wallpaper, where Charles Burchfield
worked as a designer. *Fortune* loved this city of 200,000 industrial workers who made everything from "pig iron to pretzel blenders." It even got off a joke that fixes the article in

27

its moment, and would be unthinkable today, by saying that one Buffalo company's six-ton guided bombs were "big hits in Korea."

Forty-five years and more after the fact, this article reads as a map for a lost city because so many of the sites it celebrates have slipped away. Read in a different way, the article maps another lost Buffalo, a city that never came to happen. For it notes as well that in 1946 Curtiss Wright closed its aircraft factories in the city and left 36,000 people out of work. That was an act of postwar downsizing, of closing democracy's arsenal, but that *Fortune* article added another, more troubling sentence: "Partly because Buffalo's skilled-labor reserve is growing thin, Bell is moving its helicopter division to Texas." On the screen of a microfilm reader in 1997, that simple statement was the answer I was searching for about the city, for that throwaway line from 1951 about a gimmick—a whirlybird—explained the decline of Buffalo. It was not that the city had lacked hi-tech industries, such as aircraft, but that it could not keep them when they, instead of pig iron and pretzel blenders, would become the thriving heavy manufacturers of America. The city did not start its decline in the seventies, as had always seemed the case, but rather in the late forties and early fifties, when it lost its aircraft factories. There were only three years between 1943, when Buffalo shipped more grain than any other port in history, and 1946, when its future went south. In retrospect, the city was a victim of war or, more exactly, of the peace. Either way, that celebration of Buffalo in the bible of American capitalism got its future right, that is, if you read the subtext and ignored the photographs.

Writing about Buffalo is a form of industrial archaeology. The gloomy, forbidding structures of my visits home as an adult spoke of a lost city that had faded away almost without being noticed by old residents. Yet even in abandonment these mills and elevators, these warehouses and trainyards remembered power and energy. The gentrified or new parts of the city that Buffalonians bragged about were, by contrast, on a far diminished scale: a lovely park on the harbor's edge with an expensive marina, a charming downtown theater district amid urban blight. These new sites, though, gave no clues for understanding the past of the city. That pursuit would require, in the absence of hard evidence, finding a metaphor that could hold all of the city's forms and moments in one telling phrase. That, in turn, came to me in Columbus as I read a brilliant study of industrial architecture in its glory years (1900–25) by the émigré Englishman Reyner Banham. His book bore the curious title A Concrete Atlantis and of-fered the most compelling vision of Buffalo I found in any text: it enabled me to imagine that the place was a lost city, built in the wonder material of the turn of the twentieth century, and submerged beneath a sea of history. But unlike Plato's Atlantis, or even the more skeptical Montaigne's, this site on the shore of Lake Erie would never become a mythic place in our lives, a site that demanded quest and invention, that compelled travelers to risk their lives to find it. This Atlantis was instead a site to mark that stage of American life that had passed so painfully we could only mock its ruins, with punning bad faith, as the Rust Belt.

Metaphor verges on bad faith if, through its brilliance, it pulls one's attention away from the object in question. If Buffalo were truly a concrete Atlantis, then there would be other accounts of it for me to read, other quest narratives and claims of discovery to help me make my return. But there are none. So I must decline Banham's metaphor, though I take solace from his description of the city's grain elevators:

They do have an almost Egyptian monumentality in many cases, and in abandonment and death they evoke the majesties of a departed civilization. Or so it used to seem to me, looking downstream on the Buffalo River from the angle of South Street. . . . It was a privilege to know them in their ravaged antique grandeur.

Few cities have been placed with a more severe and yet more loving accuracy than is Buffalo in this passage. For when Banham finishes with Buffalo he makes of it something far more compelling than do its apologists and boosters. His Buffalo is a site from the vernacular American past far truer—and far more painful—than any eulogized by writers on the backroads and blue highways of the sentimental traveler.

Banham's book taught one last thing about place and our relation to it: that the decay of the world we have known through our own eyes or family stories is too painful to observe. It is too much like watching our own death. That may explain why so much travel writing remembers places as they never were in fact and thus as they can survive the corrosions of time. A chronicle of place must follow Montaigne's caution about accurate description; if it tells lies, as travel books have always told lies, such a chronicle betrays its charge of remembering a vanished civilization.

The authority, even the necessity that comes with this kind of depiction of place will, in the most literal and yet revitalized sense of the cliché, hit home to natives when they encounter it. Wandering through a restored section of what had been East Berlin in the summer of 1997, I found an artfully chic gallery that was showing architectural drawings of buildings currently under construction in that city. My curiosity was entirely drawn by the future of this, to me, foreign city and so at first I failed to comprehend a sign for a show of photographs elsewhere in the gallery. It read simply, and in English, "Buffalo Grain Elevators." My failure to read that sign was a kind of cognitive dissonance, though I should have remembered more quickly than I did that German architects, especially Walter Gropius and Erich Mendelsohn, had drawn deep inspiration from Buffalo's grain elevators early in the twentieth century. These structures taught lessons about form and function that were to be applied by these architects and their disciples throughout the rest of the century.

These grain elevators were unadorned ranges of vertical cylinders placed next to each other in a beautiful, rhythmic flow. They seemed proof that the bare structure—perfect in its poured concrete form—could express an elegance beyond anything achieved by ornament. Looking back at the monuments of twentieth-century architecture that fill our cities, one can argue that the lesson of the Buffalo grain elevator was learned too well. The sterility, even the brutality of many twentieth-century buildings, though, seems all the more evident when they are set beside these elevators that have the grace of buildings that did their work well.

Those Buffalo buildings that taught the world how to be modern are long overdue for the inevitable deconstructive project, though explosives alone would be inadequate for the task. What happened to me in Berlin was an encounter with long familiar images and thus with all that they could tell about the contradictions of the place. The notion that Buffalo had once been a pilgrimage site would seem strange, even preposterous to most natives of the city. Its pride does not move in that direction, now that its elevators are marginal to this inland port. As it was, I learned this lesson through a dislocation of place, through looking at these familiar structures in a city that seemed exotic and historically overburdened to me. And more than exotic or overburdened, for that section of Berlin was nothing but one huge site of construction and reconstruction. That summer, you couldn't photograph anywhere in the center of Berlin without framing the image with construction cranes. Berlin was all about rebuilding the glories of the past and adding monuments for the future: it was about pilgrimage or, as we call it today with embarrassment, tourism. During the summer of 1997 more visitors looked at those photographs of grain elevators in Berlin than went to look at the structures themselves in Buffalo.

Viewing these photographs by Gerrit Engel in Berlin was a way of returning to Buffalo, though it was subtly affected by his decision to work in color, unlike most photographers of the Buffalo elevators who have favored black and white. Engel's choice of film, as well as the muted tones in which he printed his images, came to seem evocatively antimonumental and thus a more accurate rendering of the damage time has worked on these elevators than do those stark black-and-white images. The weathering of concrete, the peeling of sign paint, the incrustations of rust, the inscriptions of graffiti: all of these seem more prosaic in muted color than in black-and-white. Only after looking at Engel's images for a long time did I realize what made them seem accurate. The skies in his prints were not vivid blue, as in most color photos, but rather the dull white-gray of a city built along an inland sea. His prints spoke because, thousand of miles and many years from Buffalo, I saw in them the heavy sky that loomed above my childhood.

If this experience of returning home suggests a final moment, a gaze beyond further reflection because it occurred in a foreign city, then this chronicle has failed. For such a neat conclusion, with its sense of creative dislocation or geographical bricolage, belongs to another genre. My stories about Buffalo cannot end with images of the city viewed from a cosmopolitan distance but must return to North America's mediterranean. From there, one more point can be made about growing up in a provincial city: your sense of the metropole is such that you can only locate it on that same inland sea. From Trebizond you go to Constantinople, from Alexandria to Athens. To find the great city you look across the water, not behind your back across the land. For Buffalo in the late sixties that meant Toronto, not New York. Only after that first move was made could there be other metropoles.

Reading Margaret Atwood's *Cat's Eye* after it appeared in 1989 made me reimagine the Toronto I knew in the early 1970s. Further back, during the years between the opening of Atwood's novel in the 1950s and my college years, Toronto reshaped itself more self-consciously than did any other city in North America. It was not simply that it grew in numbers, but that this decorous city, whose residents had until very recently gone to Buffalo for a good time, became an entrepôt of human possibility. It became, in the phrase beloved by all civic boosters, a "world-class city," though very few of its citizens ever seemed to think then about the responsibilities carried by that label or about its costs. It was enough in the early 1970s to eat your way around the world in cheap restaurants along Bloor Street West or gaze at a numbing variety of newspapers in languages at which you could only guess. You didn't need the chamber of commerce talk to know that Toronto was an exciting place to be, though perhaps more so for an American kid like me with expatriate fantasies at the end of the Vietnam War than for a poor immigrant from Jamaica or Sicily overwhelmed by the noise and cold of the city. It was easy for me to pass. A few shifts in idiom, a passing familiarity with hockey, and some discretion about the United States went a long way toward disguising my place of origin.

At that same time, there was in Toronto another city rapidly slipping away. This other city, growing distant, had once contained a coherent culture but was by the early seventies unable, in its thinning gentility, to restrain the smelly, noisy, life-giving rush of immigration. Only after reading *Cat's Eye*, with its portrait of a receding Toronto that one might tag in shorthand British, could I identify precisely the rare moment I had sensed while living there. In a phrase that catches how things had changed, Atwood's narrator says: "Toronto didn't used to have names like Charna." No, when I lived there, it had names from nineteenth-century British novels. Atwood's portrait of that Toronto opened in memory what I did not understand at the time when I took the bus downtown from York University at the far edge of the city. The bus passed long rows of tudor houses with dark cream stucco and fussy cross-timbering, low brick apartment buildings, signs with spellings like "theatre" and "colour" that seemed more alien than those with names in Italian or Polish or with lettering in Chinese or Arabic. It was that slight dislocation—of *-re* instead of *-er*—that was exotic to an American because the difference was so understated, so easy to miss, and yet so resonant. That was the hard difference to absorb, the one that was easy to miss. Toronto spread out its lines of prim bungalows and bits of garden until, beyond its ring highway 401, a new city began: large, cheaply built apartment blocks filled with new arrivals from anywhere you could name.

The qualities celebrated in Toronto—immigrant diversity, energy, gentrification—can be found elsewhere and give no unique sense of that city, except perhaps for the intensity of their presence. In the early seventies, what made Toronto particular was that last residue of British propriety, which could not, by contrast, have been found anywhere else. Avenue Road, that marvelously named street, ran from the Royal Ontario Museum and the Park Plaza Hotel at Bloor Street to Upper Canada College, a distance of perhaps two miles, and passed through what seemed the most British part of the city. To an outsider who hardly knew the children of British Toronto, that district seemed different beyond measure from the Jewish and Greek neighborhoods where, because of my family, I felt comfortable. The houses in this district were not the largest in the city or even the most tempting. But they had a solidity, a foursquare balance that came from an absolute certainty about the order of this world. They conveyed an assurance of blood, class, and even, it might have been admitted quietly within, the glories of what had once been empire.

There was, in those last days, a sense of colonial Britishness in Toronto that still meant women in large hats and white gloves, trolley cars on main avenues, formal gardens in parks, bewigged barristers and solicitors, cars like Humbers and Sunbeams that few other countries imported, a suspicion of foreigners, tastes like digestive biscuits or vinegar on french fries, images of the queen on dollar bills too pretty to come from a northern country, a rhetorical hatred of the nation to the south then consumed by its own imperial disease in Vietnam. These were the gestures by which the old empire had kept itself from going native or turning hybrid. During the seventies as the glories of empire exhausted themselves into the confusions of commonwealth, as Toronto went native, these gestures turned ironic. The process seemed natural as I thought of my grandparents who came to the United States from Greece and Russia early in the century. It was, strange to say, Toronto as a last vestige of Anglo-Saxon virtues that remained exotic.

My friends and I took pride in being at York University rather than at the University of Toronto, in being at a raw, poured-concrete campus full of city kids, newcomers from the old empire, artsy types from the plains of Manitoba, rather than at the mock-Gothic campus of the privileged as it nestled downtown among parliament buildings and law offices on University Avenue. That university seemed to be located spiritually, as it was physically, amid the established life of the old city. If we belonged to the culture of a new Toronto eager to dispense with the protocols of empire, we gained ballast by having that old Toronto to define ourselves against. That city spoke with a voice I heard but could never register until I found it again years later in *Cat's Eye*:

> Right behind me [at an art gallery] a woman's voice says, "Well, they certainly are *different*." It's the quintessential Toronto middle-class-matron put-down, the ultimate disapproval. It's what they say about slums. It would not look good over the sofa is what she means. . . . She's convinced of her own legitimacy, her right to pronounce: I and my kind are here on sufferance.

Yes, but those who sounded this note of sufferance seemed almost impotent by the early 1970s because they were learning not only that they couldn't keep the different ones out but that they might even welcome them as barbarians at the gate. People were just beginning to read Cavafy in translation then, just beginning to wonder what he meant when he said that barbarians might be a kind of solution.

36

The women I knew in Toronto came from this older Canada, from North Bay and Burlington and Ottawa. Their charm was to be foreign in slight but seductive ways and they led me through that colonial outpost as it gave way to international port of entry. For Toronto then was something more compelling than a "world-class city" as it tried to balance the culture of British Canada with inpourings from Jamaica, Hong Kong, Kenya, and India, to name only those places where my dormmates came from. The city had never been the heart of the empire, only one place where the sun never set, but it was then the site of the most painful movement of its time. It was the place immigrants desired for its possibilities of a different life, and it in turn desired their different lives to keep itself from shrinking into obscurity. It wanted to be something more than a port city on an inland sea.

My memories of Toronto have less to do with that moment and place than with a movement between places. For that was about possibility, about crossing an inland sea toward the center of things. There was in this a great sense of freedom, which came more from leaving one place than from arriving at another. At seventeen, I was sure I was through with Buffalo: I had outgrown it and was ready for cities more exotic than the one that had raised me. I would return at times to be with my family, to remember the city that had given me some of my idiom for moving through the world. I was never ashamed of having grown up in Buffalo because it gave me a sense of the toughness of life. There was a kind of reverse glamour to saying you had grown up in Buffalo. People might feel sorry for you, but they would show a wary respect for your time in a hard place.

Toronto in the early 1970s was not the center of things, perhaps because by then there was no single center left anywhere. What was missing for me there was a sense that its past as a city of empire had left behind traces that were neither nostalgic nor tasteful. It was a city of heritage, but that word had come to mean a past one accepts without moral or, more likely, aesthetic embarrassment. It meant a usable past for interior decorators. The utter impossibility of doing that with Buffalo's past is what has made it stay with me. Looking at the world from a city in decline keeps you from believing too many of the claims other places make about their futures. And it teaches you to value those intact ruins that were once someone else's city of the future. The Queen City of the Great Lakes: Buffalo will never be that again because the economic and cultural network of that inland sea has passed.

The Buffalo of my memory has gone. The time of decline from industrial empire to Rust Belt city is, as a historical change, already in the past. The logic of geography, the inexorable power of a city well situated, should mean that Buffalo can revive itself. How that will happen, when it will happen, are puzzles beyond my telling. History has not been kind to other ports on inland seas. Trebizond, Alexandria, Trieste have never recovered their times of glory. But perhaps one can say something else about Buffalo in the company of these inland ports: that it will be named in the chronicle of places that have for a time dealt in fire and water, in the transforming elements of life.

The View from the River: Paris

Sometimes, a glimpse is enough. Later you will learn the place well, live in it, let it settle as a counterweight to home. At the moment, though, all that counts is for the place to leave its stain on the imagination. Later, you will understand that any sense of a place depends on the rush of expectation and the skepticism of memory. That first glimpse can come, as mine did of Paris, from books and pictures. There was nothing original to my sense of the city, nothing innocent.

I won't invent a memory of the first book I read about Paris, though probably it was a child's version of Dumas or Hugo that my parents gave me. But these were boys' books and they could have been set anywhere that would gratify a boy's heart. It hardly mattered then where the great sewer was, as long as it was there for that nightmarish chase scene. Now, thirty-five years and more later, I know that sewer could only have been in Paris, though I have resisted touring it as some writers urge for the sake of a historical, if not punitive, authenticity. Later in my adolescence I read nine-teenth-century French novels about young men who left the provinces for the capital. I found this story in American and Russian novels as well, in Dreiser and Turgenev, but they were not as alluring because they did not have Paris. The moment when I knew I would become less of a provincial by going to Paris came late in my teens after reading Flaubert's *Sentimental Education*. For me, that is the most Parisian of novels because it is about an outsider who is made and then unmade by Paris.

The novel opens with a glimpse, as Frédéric Moreau leaves Paris on a river steamer for his hometown of Nogent-sur-Seine: "On the 15th of September 1840, at six o'clock in the morning, the *Ville-de-Montereau* was lying alongside the Quai Saint-Bernard, ready to sail, with clouds of smoke pouring from its funnel." That Frédéric will return to Paris is inevitable, we know, because he has looked at the city along its river-run: "A long-haired man of eighteen, holding a sketchbook under his arm, stood motionless beside the tiller. He gazed through the mist at spires and buildings whose names he did not know, and took a last look at the Île Saint-Louis, the Cité, and Notre-Dame; and soon, as Paris was lost to view, he heaved a deep sigh." The sketchbook marks him as a romantic traveler intent on recording his impressions of a place.

When I first saw Paris in my late twenties, it was through the viewfinder of a 35mm camera but I was no less a romantic traveler for that. Intensely earnest, I wanted to find a place at once more sustaining and unsettling than home. It mattered in this pursuit that I went to Paris with a American woman who knew the city well and who had sufficient irony to keep reminding me that home was not so bad, that it was in fact where we lived. In time, through the geography of my marriage with her, I came to see that home was also where one wrote about elsewhere. And so I learned that one's first encounter with Paris should yield to the lingering pleasures of return, for no place is worse served by a dismissive "been there, done that."

Garish travel posters, unnerving Matisse abstractions, candy-box covers, Maigret mysteries, opening shots of all but forgotten movies—these and uncountable other images carry the great view of Paris with Notre-Dame or one of the bridges at its center. That view is also the promise Frédéric Moreau felt from the deck of his steamer. Today, we walk along the Seine, both up above it on the streets and down beside it on the quays; we walk across it on bridges that together chronicle the changing architecture of the city. Catching glimpses of it between buildings or down boulevards when we move through the city, we rarely feel distant from the Seine. Unlike rivers in New York and London, the Seine seems intimate, even comforting; it belongs to the daily rituals of life as we gaze down on it or seek a moment of rest from the city along its banks. Crossing the river in Paris does not mean, as it does elsewhere, leaving the heart of the city.

Yet something is lost to us because we can only travel the Seine as tourists on a *bateau-mouche*—Mouche being the district in Lyons where these boats were built. In the nineteenth and early twentieth centuries, Parisians rode the *bateaux-mouches* as today they ride the Métro. Annual ridership in the 1890s averaged 25 million on some 100 boats and peaked during the Exposition of 1900 at 40 million. During the first quarter of the twentieth century, the *bateaux-mouches* gradually gave way to the Métro and were finally discontinued as public transport in 1934. The French-English *Larousse* anachronistically defines "bateau-mouche" as "water-bus, passenger-steamer" when it might simply say "tourist boat."

If today *bateaux-mouches* carried Parisians between home and work, if the Seine remained a passenger artery through the body of the city, then these boats would not be scorned by veteran travelers as the waterborne equivalent of a two-hour tour through the Louvre. For years I shared that scorn, fearing above all the embarrassment of seeming an innocent American. Paris was too serious a place to be viewed from something as unoriginal as a boat that made the same circuit day in and day out with its loudspeaker squawking clichés. The *bateau-mouche* was for polyester tourists with point-and-shoot cameras, not well-read visitors like myself who loved the city for its nuances and treasured the esoteric.

I winced when I heard tourists speak of "Paris, France," lest it be confused with "Paris, Tennessee" or "Paris, Texas." They seemed, to my superior ear, so out of place and, worse yet, so utterly content to be out of place. Their Paris might as well have been a stage-set where everyone spoke English with a suggestive French accent. They leafed through American guidebooks, while I had *L'Indispensable*, the book of maps carried by every Paris cop and truckdriver. I wanted to be a *flâneur*, the wanderer through the city intent on experience and sensation rather than anything as vulgar as information. This figure, evoked by Baudelaire then canonized by Walter Benjamin and now exhausted by Edmund White, had a purity that made him (always him!) superior to everyone else on the street. In his distaste for the obvious, the *flâneur* was exquisitely nostalgic, though one could sometimes wonder if he knew anything about the obvious except to shun it. The *flâneur* was, though, a role easily played by young men whose reading had made them fastidious and prematurely aged.

Writing about Paris the temptation is always to evade the obvious, because overobserved, and instead concentrate on the hidden, the esoteric, the eccentric. Perhaps the native Parisian can write such a book successfully, but the outsider who tries to do so is doomed to mistaking the trivial for the profound. That Paris is the most touristic of places, the most evoked in prose both purple and plain, makes avoiding the clichés about the place the greatest cliché of all. What then? Abandon Paris, head for parts unwritten, cultivate a taste for adventure travel? As I came to understand that tourists remain tourists as a form of protection, as their ticket home, I also realized that the way to write Paris was to follow their lead. For as they rode the *bateau-mouche*, they could see something about the history of the city that escaped me in my snobbish pretense of being a traveler.

For the view along the river from, roughly, Pont Mirabeau in the west to Pont d'Austerlitz in the east allows Paris to reveal the shape it has made for itself over time. The pace of the *bateau-mouche*, slower and more continuous than the city traffic, allows you to think about the course that river has taken. And here we reach a paradox about tourism. The better I knew Paris and its streets, the more learned my knowledge of the city became, the more I had to become a tourist on a *bateau-mouche* to complete my education. For only in that way could I trace the city's main artery. Yet this kind of travelogue had to be more than a transcription of immediate experience. There had to be a place in it for all the books and images about Paris that had circulated in my mind. Between the *flâneur* and the tourist there could be a way to write Paris that was neither too knowing nor too innocent. This travelogue was the form for writing about Paris because it would also register the elegiac quality of the city, its layers of history as they are at once contained in

45

buildings or monuments and as they elude those forms of official memory.

The tape on *La Flute* (two levels, one thousand seats, room enough for perhaps twenty busloads of tourists) runs through five languages in fixed sequence: French, English, German, Italian, and Spanish. The order expresses the local hierarchy. There is no Asian language. The content of each soundbite varies slightly from language to language. The French is densely and precisely didactic, the German seems edited to elide certain historical awkwardnesses, the English sounds the most elementary. The tape cycles endlessly, with a brief horn-blast between segments to keep the languages from running into each other and to remind us to follow the lecture. On a warm evening in the early spring, the light suffusing Paris leaves me content and disinclined to listen. I've read too many books about Paris to need this lecture, I think, and drift off into memories of Balzac and Proust, only to be brought back to the present by the loudspeaker identifying the penthouse apartment of a fashion designer. It strikes me that such a detail would find its way into their novels if they were writing today, for both understood the force of celebrity when writing about Paris. From the *bateau-mouche*, though, the sights remain distinct; they are too rich in image, story, language to flow together seamlessly on the first circuit around the river. And so I cherish momentary, partial views from the river—the views of the visitor, not the resident, the happy tourist on a boat.

Start with the bridges. They should be seen not merely from oblique angles along the banks but head-on from the river. Most of their names are descriptive—Neuf, Petit, Royal—or commemorative: Alexandre III, Invalides, Alma, Austerlitz, Sully. These bridges form an encyclopedia of ways to span a river. There are now about twenty-five of them across the Seine within the old city limits, and each marks out a stage in its history. The city has been shaped and reshaped by the placement of a bridge: the flow of traffic shifts, a row of neglected buildings reemerges into view, the scene takes on a different aspect when glimpsed from halfway across a new span. The narrowness of the Seine makes crossing the river a kind of interlude from the streets, a brief moment of blue that eases the beiges and grays of the city's buildings.

The last of the floating piscines in central Paris, just east of the bridge that joins the Place de la Concorde and the Assemblée National, advertised itself as "La Plage de Paris." Now, when Parisians prefer the beaches of Dakar and Cancun, this swimming pool on a barge was as much a relic as a Deux Cheveaux Citröen and has been towed away. I had hoped that it would, in time, have met the honorable fate of Parisian monuments and become a museum with photomurals of old steamers and floating laundries, with newspaper clippings of suicides pulled from the river and taken to the morgue on the Île de la Cité, with cross-section views of working barges, and with a few of those old stalls filled with junk and occasional treasures that rest on the parapets above the river. In my fantasy, I would moor this river museum to the Pont de la Concorde that was made from stones taken from the demolished Bastille. The French passion for history is never far from their sense of thrift.

The frieze of the Gare d'Orsay repeats the decorative motif "Paris—Orleans | | PO." As long as that inscription remains, the building will keep some of the enormous self-confidence it had as a railroad station built for the Exposition of 1900. Now, as a museum, it stands pompous and lost, its enormous musculature wasted on painting, sculpture,

47

furniture. It was meant for dramatic rituals of arrival and departure, realized most hauntingly in the return of French prisoners from Nazi camps. In *The War*, Marguerite Duras tells of her wait for the train that would bring her lover back from captivity in the East. In the late spring of 1945, the station built for the tourist trade of 1900 found a monumental purpose beyond the dreams of any architect. But one can only see that moment in the history of the Gare d'Orsay by having read Duras.

Today the Seine is so channelled, so guided by stonework that it takes imagination to see that once it could flood much of the city because it was not safely below the level of the streets. In the past, travel and trade along the Seine could be halted for as many as eight months of the year because of flood or drought. Now, with most traffic into and out of the city carried by motor vehicles, the Seine seems a kind of riverine margin for the highway—the Voie Georges Pompidou—that runs parallel to it along some of its quays. With the river course set so low, the cornices of buildings along the quays are more visible from the boat than are their doorways. One only sees people as they use spaces—quays, walkways, steps, bridges, esplanades—that are defined by their relation to the river. I wait for those moments when, from the *bateau-mouche*, the streets and cars and buses disappear from sight. Just for a moment, Paris becomes a great maritime city from an earlier century. And then, to wake me from rhapsodizing there appears a gravel barge as foulsmelling as any dumptruck. The river is still a place for work, still connected to the Atlantic and, through a web of canals and waterways, to the remainder of the continent.

The Pont Neuf is the oldest surviving bridge in Paris; its two sections were begun in 1578 and finished in 1604. During the spring of 1990, the municipal authorities were

48

rebuilding the quay at water level, pile-driving steel beams into the riverbed to reinforce the retaining wall of the quay and of the bridge above. The work was being done by diesel equipment chained to barges and painted a wildly discordant orange. Yet even amid this machinery, the Pont Neuf remained the bridge that Laurence Sterne mocked so affectionately in *A Sentimental Journey* of 1768: "Of all the bridges which ever were built, the whole world who have passed over the *Pont Neuf* must own, that it is the noblest— the finest—the grandest—the lightest—the longest—the broadest that ever conjoined land and land together upon the face of the terraqueous globe." There is, as this scene of reconstruction shows, very little in central Paris that is purely old or purely new; there is the built and the rebuilt, the converted and the recycled. The ways in which thrift and a sense of the past have shaped Paris seem strikingly alien to an American whose experience of cities is marked by a fast flourishing followed by decline, by the loss of a center and the seepage of life into suburbs. If Paris can seem at times too preserved, too heavily coated with maquillage, it rarely seems a place of rank decay or abandonment.

The Palais de Justice that looms over the river from the Île de la Cité is, like most public buildings in Paris, guarded by paramilitary cops who cradle submachine guns. This display of firepower, so much more intimidating than any you see in a more mythically dangerous American city like Detroit, belongs to Paris as the capital of riots and barricades, of wide boulevards built on the diagonal so that they could be swept clean by fire from well-placed artillery. In order to rebuild or, more precisely, to defuse a revolution-torn Paris in the mid-nineteenth century, Baron Haussmann drew on the baroque axial plan that was first used in the great hunting parks of the late medieval aristocracy. In both settings, diagonals radiating from a central point cut across otherwise impenetrable spaces, whether urban or rural, and make for more efficient lines of fire. Assertions of power are everywhere in the public form of Paris; the city has been designed to seize vantage points and lines of sight. The river is not part of the planned city. Indeed, in its disorderliness, its cutting across these diagonals at strange angles of its own, the Seine can sometimes remind you of the earlier Paris that Haussmann worked so hard to suppress.

Haussmann's diagonals also offered a new way to see and represent the patterns of urban life. The most knowing student of Paris's diagonals is Gustave Caillebotte who, in the 1870s, used them to structure his paintings. In a picture of three men scraping the thin boards of a hardwood floor, now at the Musée d'Orsay, Caillebotte tilts the angle of representation so that the angle of new city boulevards becomes a way to see the familiar interior of a Parisian house. In a painting of public space, like *Paris, A Rainy Day* or, more obviously, *Le Pont de l'Europe*, Caillebotte fills the canvas with the geometry of Haussmann's Paris. As a couple walks across this bridge over the railyards at the Gare Saint-Lazare, a man leans down to look at the scene below through the spaces formed by the diagonal ironwork of the bridge. In a brilliant shift of perspective, Caillebotte uses the politically-inspired geometry of the grand boulevards to portray that most Parisian of customs, enjoying the view from a bridge. His modern gesture—modern, that is, for his moment—was to have that bridge cross a railroad rather than a river. Thinking about his way of seeing Paris, I remember that I first saw a painting by Caillebotte in Buffalo, a city that was young and thriving in its industrial power when he painted this bridge.

50

Where would strollers crossing Parisian bridges be without a *bateau-mouche* to stare down at—that favorite vantage of Parisians? As tourists on the boat, we complete the scene by giving the others someone to look down on. We become part of the economy of native and visitor, resident and tourist. With great stylized pleasure, one young man gestures obscenely at a tourist on our boat photographing him and his friends as they sit on a stair running down to the river. The irony, though, is on him. His gesture does not spoil the tourist's photograph but rather makes it perfect by adding a touch of that Gallic lawlessness that drew us to Paris in the first place. The gesture satisfies the tourist's need for an experience that is disruptive, though never threatening. We become for each other the desired object of difference. They provide us with the local color we search for as tourists, and we provide them with the authenticity they fear losing as residents.

In Archbishop's Square, at the eastern end of the Île de la Cité behind Notre-Dame, there is a Mémorial de la Déportation for the French who were expatriated by the Nazis and died in the camps. Here was one of the divergences in the tape on the *bateau-mouche*. The section in German passed over this detail quickly and not, one suspects, out of good manners, but rather out of a memory of Hitler's order, unheeded but still terrifying, that Paris be burned as German troops retreated. I wish in retrospect that I had been alert enough at this moment to watch others on the boat to see what they made of this memorial. For this is one of the few sites along the river where history remains raw and unsanctified by time, that has not been polished by writers. In the early evening, the memorial lay in the shadows cast by the two towers of Notre-Dame and seemed marked as sacred space, as touched by that mercy Paris has always sought from

51

the Virgin. As I looked at the memorial from the river, though, the balance shifted. Notre-Dame remains the holy center of Paris not because of her name or faith but because she shadows this memorial. She seems now to have been touched by the atrocities of the twentieth century.

The only building to break the plane of rooflines along the Left Bank—a symmetry not of absolute regularity but of stylistic affinity—is the Tour d'Argent, the restaurant famous for serving duck to wealthy diners. From its huge plate-glass windows on the upper stories it is said to offer the finest view of Notre-Dame in all of the city, and perhaps it does. But what diners see from there is only a building, not a site of memory and mercy. It is better to contemplate Notre-Dame from the river where lush and twisted ivy grows over the parapets. That view of the cathedral has a piety that comes with time and water.

The enormous buildings of the Université Pierre et Marie Curie—Paris VI & VII—built in the mid 1960s, but already shabby, also break the symmetry of style along the Left Bank. For the run of the river westward from the Maison de l'ORTF, the headquarters of the national radio and television services, in the sixteenth arrondissement through to this point, these are the first modern constructions fully visible from the Seine. This site was earlier occupied by the wine-markets of Paris, wine being perhaps the most valuable bulk cargo to be shipped on the medieval Seine. Here too is the Quai Saint-Bernard where Frédéric Moreau embarked on the *Ville-de-Montereau* and steamed upriver (that is, southeast) to Nogent-sur-Seine. He thus would have had his last view of Notre-Dame that morning looking aft as, I like to imagine, he sketched the city receding into the morning distance. That sketch was a pledge of return.

From the *bateau-mouche* that early evening, I saw a very different sight. On the embankment at the eastern end of the Île Saint-Louis several men—aggressively masculine, even for the French, in their shirtlessness—were catching the last of the evening sun. The spaces along the river have become through custom an erotic zone. They combine privacy, because they are below the flow of traffic, with a measure of display all the more alluring for being aimed at those beyond touch, at those of us on boats or the opposite bank of the river.

As it rounded the Île Saint-Louis and headed back west, the *bateau-mouche* stopped and reversed itself to yield right-of-way to two working barges lashed together: the *Valerianne* and the boastfully named *Je Fais Causer*. And it did set my tongue to talk, with its laundry hung out to dry on the line and a little white Peugeot 205 on the aft deck. These barges seem at once the most cosily domestic of boats and the most intrepidly adventurous. They look stubby and graceless beside the streamlined, modernistic *bateaux-mouches*, but they would have the advantage over the long haul if one were to go down the Seine. Near them, the *bateaux-mouches* seem utterly Parisian in their stylish fragility; their look does not travel well but it is perfect for this stretch of the river.

From the upper deck of the *bateau-mouche*, one can catch a sudden glimpse of the roof ducts of the Pompidou Center. Amid the dull stonework of the surrounding buildings, these metal fixtures are shocking in their hard primary colors. From the glassed-in lower deck, you cannot see this imposition on the old city, one tolerated only because it is a museum. That glimpse, precisely because fleeting and possible only from the river, reveals the secret of the Parisian palette: subdue the background with the beiges and grays of stone buildings and then accent with colors in rich, lead-based enamels. The large gateways into courtyards and the win-dow shutters of buildings are painted in these shades of red, blue, and green. With their toxic allure, these enamels do not appear on the charts of American paint stores. The red, for instance, seems a compound of equal parts beaujolais and blood. This palette of subdued background and intense accent is also favored by Parisian women of a certain age.

Île de la Cité. The most resonant phrase in the French language. The tape tells us that it has been settled since prehistoric times because it was situated at a natural cross-roads. The Egyptian hieroglyph for a city was a circle wrap-ping around a cross, a wall enclosing a crossroads. To that wonderful image one might add a meandering, bisecting line for the river and thus draw a hieroglyph specific to Paris. Topography ensured that this island would have had its his-tory long before Cité or any other name for it appeared in the written record. As is immediately evident to anyone with an eye for terrain, to anyone who can see that it is shaped triumphantly like a great ship heading downstream astride the flow of the river, this island was never before history. Now, with its crowds and weathered buildings, it is hard to look at the island and see it as a place that was once so new it had yet to compel human settlement. But the chance to imagine for a moment a river view without the city is itself reason to make the trip along the Seine.

Looking from *La Flute* toward a boat belonging to another line, the Velettes du Pont Neuf, I see that both are stylized like spaceships or racing cars, all sharp angles and swoopy curves. One of the few visible touches of modernity in cen-tral Paris, these boats have by now acquired that dated look of objects born in the full, streamlined flush of twentieth-century optimism. Like the unmistakable shark-profile of the Citröen DS, these boats belong to the French recovery from World War II. When this style comes to seem old-fashioned, the *bateaux-mouches* will strike a classic note in the view. Now they lack the functional elegance of machines that have done their work well over generations. They have yet to earn the idiosyncratic names of the barges—*Falstaff, La Chatte, Jopi, Mermot, Christine G*—names that make me wonder about what it might be like to live and work on these inland waterways.

The tape on the tour boat does not call attention to these river barges. We are on vacation; we do not want to hear of those who work on the Seine. Nor of those, worse still, who die in it. Yet the drowned belong in any view of a great city's river. The loveliest bridge in Paris, the Pont des Arts with its pedestrian traffic crossing to and from the Louvre, belongs to the irreducible anecdote of the urban novel as Balzac invented it in the 1830s with *Le Peau de Chagrin*:

> Every suicide is a poem sublime in its melancholy. Where will you find, emerging from the ocean of literature, a book that can vie in genius with a news-item such as:
>
> *Yesterday, at four o'clock, a woman threw herself into the Seine from the Pont des Arts.*

When the novel of city life turned soft and became a sentimental portrait of bohemian Paris, as in George Du Maurier's *Trilby* of 1894, the Pont des Arts could provide the setting for the heartfelt musings of its three English protagonists: "When they reached the Pont des Arts they would cross it, stopping in the middle to look up the river towards the old Cité and Notre Dame, eastward, and dream unutterable things, and try to utter them." These moments of urban despair and dilettantish romanticism are not as far apart as they might seem; at times, only a franc or two separated them. Now, both moments belong to the repertoire of images that draw us to Paris and, more immediately, to its river. They are part of our sentimental education.

On another of the tourist boats, one of the hands is so obviously bored by the view that he sits backwards and separates himself from all those who eagerly look forwards. It is a stylized gesture that belongs to the economy of native and visitor. He looks away from the view enforced by the running commentary over the speakers; he mocks that endlessly cycling voice, in fact, by looking at something other than what it commands him to look at. That is another view from the river: discordant, out-of-synch with the official version, utterly Parisian. It takes longer for an American, indeed for any outsider, to learn that gesture.

The Pont d'Alma, named for a French victory in the Crimean War, bears on one of its piers the statue of a nineteenth-century Algerian Zouave. This colonial guards the capital city both symbolically and literally, for the flood-level of the Seine is measured by how deeply the Algerian is submerged beneath the rising water. This measure is so much a part of Parisian life that the Michelin Guide scruples to note that the highest water occurred in January 1910 when the Seine rose to the Zouave's chin. That this fantasy of a faithful colonial retainer who refuses to yield his position even in the face of certain death can be realized only in stone; that this dream of empire which, as it died in Indochina and North Africa, almost destroyed France with it; that Parisian bridges must serve the commemorative function of obelisks in ancient empires—all of this and more could be the substance for a deconstructive study of the Zouave on the bridge. More telling is to note that today many compatriots of that colonial soldier are Parisian cops.

The Eiffel Tower looms, as does Notre-Dame further to the east, over the river. It has its place in the aesthetic of

Paris as the monument to a romance that began in derision and endures in devotion. The tower has been used as a platform for overseas radio broadcasts since 1907; the first message was to the colonial city of Casablanca. That it took so long after the tower's erection in 1889 for society to find its function reminds us that truly visionary constructions seem useless until the pragmatic view of life can turn them to its own ends. Or that, with a broadcast platform as magnificent as the Eiffel Tower awaiting it, radio was inevitable.

An old boat, perhaps a river steamer of the type no longer used in Paris, is moored to the Right Bank. It is now the "Shogun—Restaurant Japonais." Yes, and once the Eiffel Tower bore huge illuminated signs to fill the night sky with the name of Citröen. Use and reuse, history and thrift, all of this can seem perplexing to a North American looking at the city.

Down the middle of the Seine at this point runs Swan Alley, a knife-edge made of stonework and masonry. There the bodies of murdered Protestants drifted after the St. Bartholomew's Day Massacre of August 24, 1572, when the Seine, as stories have it, ran red with their blood. Violence, both from within and without, is the history of Paris. Writing of the physical sensations of Paris, Henry James caught them exactly: "They were the smell of revolution, the smell of the public temper—or perhaps simply the smell of blood." It is the outsider, the bookish American novelist attuned to his own nation's smell of violence, who gets the sensation exactly. Those who lived through the events of 1968 in Paris must catch that smell from time to time.

The Atlantic is now, the tape tells us, 350 kilometers away. That is the distance Viking raiders traveled in November 885 when they besieged Paris for a full year. There were bridges in Paris then, and only after they were damaged by battle and flood were the Vikings able to pass through the city. Paris was not at that time the political or religious center of France or the Holy Roman Empire. This siege demonstrated forever that the city was at the heart of the waterways—the Marne, Seine, and Yonne—that give central France its coherence. This new map that forever afterwards put Paris at its center was a Viking legacy.

At the end of Swan Alley is a small version of the Statue of Liberty. The dates inscribed on the pages of Liberty's open book—July 4, 1776 and July 14, 1789—commemorate revolutions too disparate to be honored by the same monument. Yet now as Paris becomes a postcolonial city filled with refugees and immigrants from Africa and Asia as well as Eastern Europe, this statue has begun to have for Parisians the same meaning it has long had for Americans. As the New World provides the Old with a story to understand immigration, the statue becomes a different kind of monument. When my father's book on the life of East European Jews in New York City, *World of Our Fathers*, was translated in 1997 as *Le Monde de Nos Pères*, French reviewers read it as a parable about immigration and neglected its engagement with New York City. If that Statue of Liberty stood in a Paris airport as a sign of welcome, then it would speak more eloquently of French experience at the end of the twentieth century.

A sense of difference becomes overwhelming as you see on the Left Bank along the Front de Seine the tall, new hotels where factories, including that of Citröen, once stood. These hotels have the placeless names of international tourism: Nikko, Flatotel. They would be characterless failures in New York, Mexico City, or Hong Kong, but here they seem repellent because they break the harmonious roofline of buildings along the Seine. From this point to the far, eastern end of the Île Saint-Louis, Paris is an old city of cream or grayish stone relieved by enamelled trim and bright awnings. Beyond these limits, the city spreads out its steel and glass newness, the interchangeable style of modern cities that appears in central Paris only as the tower looming above the Gare Montparnasse. Like the city planners of Paris, those who write the tape for the *bateau-mouche* know that we do not want to see these steel and glass structures because they do not figure in our capital of memory and expectation. To see that city, we ride the boats of the Circle Line and read books like Jan Morris's *Manhattan '45*.

We pass more barges—*Kesara, Baltic, Shantif, Danton, Cigogne*—and then a smallish building on the Left Bank belonging to the Port Autonome de Paris. That is the sign I have unconsciously been seeking all along because, with the pedantry of the French bureaucrat, it establishes Paris as the autonomous port, the place of entry that defines its own limits, that controls the incursion of outsiders.

The Eiffel Tower appears again and again in this view from the river, and each time seems yet more immense. From this lower vantage it gains the scale it lacks at street-level where the surrounding buildings press against it insistently. From the river, where these buildings cannot be seen, the tower soars upward in an unbroken lyric curve. It is this shift of perspective from the river that proves Roland Barthes's observation about the tower: that to climb it is "to accede to a *view*"; even more, it is to celebrate the idea of a bird's-eye view that enables one to see the shape of the city. The Eiffel Tower is a monument to our desire to see anew all that surrounds us in even the most familiar of landscapes. Like the *bateau-mouche*, though from a higher vantage, the Tower allows us to look anew at the ground level we usually occupy.

The last barges we passed that evening seemed wistfully named: *Tyrol, Errant, Siam.* These boats, bound to the low-land waterways of Europe, express that yearning to be else-where, in romantic other-regions far beyond the established circuit, that we assume belongs only to those who are fixed immovably in their home place. Those who make their homes on barges can still dream of elsewhere.

The final scene: as *La Flute* pulls up alongside another *bateau-mouche*, a tourist on that boat takes a photograph of us coming in. The visual loop complements the audio loop and gives our journey a ceremonial quality. Everything cir-cles without closure, everything becomes part of memory. "The Seine, which was a yellowish colour, had risen almost to the level of the bridges. It was giving off a chilly breath. Frédéric filled his lungs with it, savouring that wonderful Paris air which seems to contain exhalations of both love and intelligence." Thus Flaubert describes Frédéric, now a grown man long resident in Paris, on his return to the city after a visit to his family in Nogent.

The characteristic modern view of the city is not from the river but from the air. Taken directly overhead from a height far higher than any human construction could reach, the aerial photograph simplifies the texture of the city by focus-ing on streets, roof tops, routes of flow, grids, uses of available space, constraints of rock or water as they shape a place. These photographs deprive the city of its people, its archi-tectural details, its shifting flows of light and dark, its mo-ments of intimacy, neighborhood, eccentricity—all of the complaints expressed by modernist writers bound within London, Paris, Berlin, Saint Petersburg. The aerial image joins the new technologies of flight and photography to the modernist despair of the city; the result is a vision of the city as an inhuman grid entrapping its inhabitants, or as a target waiting to be bombed.

The earlier vantage from on-high, the bird's-eye view, does not destroy human texture because it is oblique rather than perpendicular to the city. Its elevation is measured in hundreds, rather than thousands, of feet and allows for the play of detail, of human movement among buildings, along streets, in green spaces and beside water. Topographically, the bird's-eye was available from a cliff or high hill; architecturally, in the premodern world from the religious vantage of pyramid, dome, tower, or spire. In Paris, it was from the thirteenth century the view from Notre-Dame, a vantage that compels us to see the city as sacred space ordered through the same faith that is worshipped in the building on which one stands. To ascend to this view of Paris from the towers of Notre-Dame is to partake for a moment in God's vision of the city, or so it must have seemed at a time when one could look down only from a religious structure. The Eiffel Tower and later the skyscrapers in La Défense had to be built before Parisians could have a secular view of their city.

No view in Paris is as privileged as that from Notre-Dame. That view atop the island in the Seine has always drawn tourists, once called pilgrims, but also Parisians of the most unlikely sort. Thus the bohemians Marcel and Rudolph in Henri Murger's *Scénes de la vie de Bohème* (1851) count as an extravagance during a rare moment of prosperity "the day [they] went up the Notre Dame tower to have a bird's eye view of Paris" at the cost of eight sous. (It cost them, by comparison, one sou each to cross the Pont des Arts.) The view from the towers of Notre-Dame has become an image on millions of postcards and tourist photographs; each must include in silhouette against the Seine far below one of the gargoyles that decorate the tower. These details fix the view

61

in a code unique to the site: medieval grotesque set against the river.

So established is this view in our repertoire of images that it hit me as a terrible shock, as a moment of positive turned to negative, to see Brassaï's photographs taken from the tower of Notre-Dame—at night. The gargoyles are there in dense black silhouette but the usual painterly arrangement of light and dark in the view, of bright sky and dull buildings, has been reversed by these brilliant revisionary photographs: the sky is dark, the buildings luminous from within. These photographs give the pleasure that comes of a stunning new view from the most clichéd of vantage points.

Brassaï's photographs from Notre-Dame and Barthes's mythology of the Eiffel Tower are both attempts to define the urban view from on high. What joins them is the Seine because, as it bisects the city topographically and culturally, it poses the persistent question of perspective: what is it that we learn from this vantage? How does this one view enlarge the sense we carry about with us of a place, a composite made up of people, buildings, greenspaces, water, old songs, smells, palette, conveyances, foods, images, and the rest? These are questions that a writer about place must continually ask because each yields answers only to those who return to look again and again.

Writing of the view from the Seine, John Russell has observed that "Paris is the only city in which a great river has been used for mile after mile, on right bank and left, as the natural center of a work of art." Such monuments as the Louvre, the Gare d'Orsay, the Jeu de Paume, the Orangerie, and a bit further in, Cluny originally defined themselves in relation to the Seine, for no assertion of political, spiritual, or technological power could be made without reference to the vital river-run. In its moment, each of these buildings was at the heart of the city. Now each survives, bereft of its original purpose, as a museum presenting Paris as a cultural artifact. The trains depicted in the paintings found in the upper galleries of the Musée d'Orsay accepted and discharged passengers in the great halls below when it was the Gare d'Orsay. The liturgical objects, tapestries, and pilgrims' medals that gave medieval people their sense of place now stand displayed in the rooms of the Cluny. The endlessly complex interchange between political power and art writes its own history in the Louvre, from the trophies of conquest and colonialism hanging on its walls to the erection of I. M. Pei's pyramid in the late 1980s. Each building asserts the continuing presence of the past because each is no more than a brief walk from the Seine.

Only one building along the river remains unchanged. Notre-Dame is still consecrated ground, the church of the archbishop of Paris. Yet unlike at Chartres, praying or even lighting a candle in this cathedral feels anachronistic. It seems more appropriate to observe it with a camera. So, in an oblique, ambivalent way, Notre-Dame belongs with this series of buildings along the river that have yielded their original purpose to the current moment. The Eiffel Tower, that nineteenth-century celebration of industrial optimism, now stands as an obelisk to its time.

To find the view from the river requires historical imagination because it clashes with our way of seeing cities from above. Yet the view from the Seine, or from the Thames or the Mississippi, defines the place because it reminds us that one location along the river's run was settled because it was most fertile to the imagination. And then there appeared markets for all of the essential tradegoods: grain, wine, sex, paintings, ideas, languages, visitors. In V. S. Pritchett's *London Perceived*, the run of the Thames gives structure to the chaotic history of the place. Canny writer that he is, Pritchett expects us always to hear behind his own prose the opening of Conrad's *Heart of Darkness* as Marlow evokes the earliest history of London by remembering that the Thames estuary has also been "one of the dark places of the earth." For Conrad's narrator to reach the great river of the Congo he must begin with the Thames, for that was the site of the empire-building worked by Europeans on each other in past centuries. The river is, again, the connecting flow across distances of time and place. The Thames has always been a river of danger for novelists, a place that has become, in Jonathan Raban's chilling observation, "the supreme symbol of London the city—a place where it is easy to drown."

The American view from the river can seem far removed from the limits of history. When Huck and Jim raft down the Mississippi, the town that signals the junction with the Ohio River—and thus the crucial turn to the north and freedom—is Cairo, but it passes by in the night unseen. Later, St. Louis is no more than a scattering of lights. The city has no place in this narrative of the river because it is about the need, in Huck's closing words, "to light out for the territory." No metal arch along the river's edge can match that eloquence. Through the view from another American river, Walt Whitman asserts the soul's transcendence over the facts of time and place; he speaks in *Crossing Brooklyn Ferry* of cutting across the East River, rather than of flowing along it, in order to cancel the old metaphor of time as a river that flows endlessly and estranges us from each other:

It avails not, time nor place—distance avails not,
I am with you, you men and women of a generation, or ever so
    many generations hence,
Just as you feel when you look on the river and sky, so I felt.

All will change, as Whitman knows, except the presence of the river but that alone will ensure communion across time. This is not a poem one could write looking across the Seine; the scale along that river is too intimate. Its reminders of the past impress on us that connections across time and space belong to history rather than the transcendent soul. But this reading of Whitman's poem, and the great American rivers that flow through it, became possible to me only after I thought about what it meant to travel on the Seine, to engage the city as a capital.

Journey, story, and metaphor alike draw from the same need: to move from point to point in the hope of discovery. Journey narratives and metaphors share at least this same ambiguous orientation; they move between the known and the unknown in ways that simple linearity or the overly precise grid cannot render. They move back and forth between their points; departure is not forgotten on arrival, arrival prompts memories of departure. The circuits traced by *La Flute* and other tour boats in great river-cities follow this rhythm. They move us along the element of time so that we can find a view of the city that, unlike others that impose a static clarity from above, allows us to feel how the city has shaped its history through its natural setting.

If, from afar, a great city seems fixed in its site, residents know that its periphery is never set but always shifting along paths of least resistance. Those with long memories can remember when the city's focal area—its agora, crossroad, suk, downtown—was elsewhere. But these internal changes rarely concern travelers as they approach the city from a distance. To them, geography remains valid not by providing a route from periphery to center but by corresponding to their own imagination of a place. When Montesquieu wrote his *Persian Letters* (1721) and established the necessary fiction of viewing one's home place through the eyes of the outsider, he understood that the traveler's misconceptions can be more telling than the inhabitant's knowledge. Here, in a letter sent back to Persia from Leghorn, Usbek outlines his journey and its logic. His greatest insight lies in what the resident would consider a laughable error: "Rica and I plan to go immediately to Paris, which is the capital of the empire of Europe. Travellers always seek out the big cities, which are a sort of common homeland for every foreigner." Paris as the common homeland of travelers could be a book in itself, especially if it extracted from travelers' tales all those observations that would most perplex the natives of the city. Usbek's characterization of Paris as the "capital of the empire of Europe" predicts Napoleon's vision of European empire and also the city's place as the capital, in Walter Benjamin's phrase, of the nineteenth century.

Montesquieu's tactic in the *Letters* proves the value of foreign knowledge. That there is worth in the outsider's response is, of course, the implicit claim made by journey narratives, portraits of place, imagined cities, meditations on landscape. Yet foreign knowledge must also draw on previous encounters with the place, whether through books or pictures or anything else that provokes in the viewer a necessary sense of expectation. This sense of the river and the *bateau-mouche* as ways of viewing Paris belong for me with Fernand Braudel's advice "to be on the lookout for divergences, contrasts, breaks, frontiers." I suspect few Parisians would think of the Seine as a break or frontier in their city, except as it obviously demarcates the two very different forms of the city labeled Right Bank and Left Bank. But the idea of the Seine as a break or frontier is tantalizing for those who would view the city as the accretion of history in a particular site defined by its geography.

That human places are fixed in their topography means travelers will depict them in terms taken from those who have come before. There is, typically, a sequence that runs from one writer's brilliant invention to later writers' knowing, and then increasingly tired, allusions to the original remark. English travelers to Paris between about 1820 and 1920 seemed unable to resist the wonderful opening of Laurence Sterne's *Sentimental Journey*: "They order, said I, this matter better in France—." The matter may not be specified but the journey to France follows immediately afterwards, as do the narrator's amorous adventures in postchaises and other very un-English sites. I have no idea how many later writers actually quoted this sentence of Sterne's but a few examples prove the point.

Fanny Trollope, best known for her acid portrait of the United States, traveled to Paris in the summer of 1835 and wrote a book in the form of letters home meant to assure the English that the dangerous influence of radical politicians and writers (as exemplified by Hugo and Balzac, of whose *La Peau de Chagrin* she wrote: "IT WILL NOT LAST"), was on the wane in Paris and certainly would not survive to infect their country. In the midst of this wildly mistaken assessment of France, she observes the city from a stiffly Tory vantage. She climbs the tower of Notre-Dame and speculates about the river and this "magnificent capital which has so strangely chosen to stretch herself along its banks"; that is, which has not patterned itself on London's use of the Thames as a port. Anything that deviates from the British model, even the Seine, seems dangerous to her. Her vision

67

of Paris, at once wary and condescending, is characterized perfectly by her artful rewriting of Sterne's sentence: "Here again I may quote the often-quoted, and say, 'They manage all these matters differently at least, if not better, in France.'" Years later when the ideas that horrified Mrs. Trollope had become sufficiently acceptable to attract the British to Paris, George Du Maurier describes one of his characters in *Trilby* (1894) looking into the window of a patisserie on the Rue Castiglione: "the Laird, who was well read in his English classics and liked to show it, would opine that 'they managed these things better in France.'" Arthur Bartlett Maurice, whose *The Paris of the Novelists* (1919) is most memorable for never once mentioning Flaubert's *Sentimental Education*, observed sententiously that since Sterne wrote *A Sentimental Journey* with its memorable opening, "English men of letters of all conditions and degrees of talent have been turning to the near-by land for direct inspiration and for occasional background."

The underrated travel writer E. V. Lucas (1913) caught this habit of quoting Sterne perfectly by speaking of that opening sentence "which no other writer on Paris has succeeded in forgetting." Perhaps English writers on Paris still feel compelled to quote Sterne to prove themselves sentimental travelers, as beings more receptive to experience than mere tourists. I doubt it, though. Sterne now sounds curiously arch because more recent writers have specified the matter better-ordered in France. Something vital went out of English writing on Paris when the allusion to Sterne became limited to sex—a sense that France, and more especially Paris, could satisfy any of our desires because there all matters are better-ordered. At the very least, though, Sterne's sentence with its alluring promise sent more than a few readers off to Paris. As for what they found, that was largely a matter of what their reading told them they would find there. With Sterne's sentence, they inherited a view of Paris.

This travelogue of a trip on a *bateau-mouche* in the 1990s is fixed in its own moment. It renders a Paris self-consciously idealizing itself through the preservation of its past. The defining quality of central Paris along the run of the *bateaux-mouches* is that it outlaws the defining feature of the modern city: tall buildings made of glass, steel, concrete. This absence is not the result of some preference for aesthetics over finances; rather it places value on a well-preserved central city without towering buildings. Puns on the word *capital* should probably be avoided but they do capture how the city has identified the source of its long-term wealth.

This process of capitalizing Paris has of necessity altered the history of the city by removing sights that would offend or trouble visitors. Perhaps the most obvious sight missing from the quays of the Seine today is the large number of *clochards*—no English "bum" or "derelict" or "down-and-out" captures the resonances of the French—that once lived beneath the bridges of Paris. In his *Secret Paris of the Thirties*, Brassaï includes several moving and mysterious photographs of the clochards at night. His true memorial to them, though, is this passage written many years later after their numbers had (and this is his comparison) shrunk like Balzac's *La Peau du Chagrin*: "To awake at dawn beside the Seine to the sounds of the birds and roosters in the seed stores along the Quai de la Mégisserie, to enjoy the sunrise behind Notre Dame and the sunset behind the Grand Palais or the Trocadéro, was the envied privilege this group, officially listed as S.D.F.—*Sans domicile fixe*, without permanent residence—enjoyed, since they had sacrificed everything for their freedom." By conventional standards, the clochards were dirty, often drunk, homeless, everything that tourists avoid in their own countries. Their presence was troubling to the authorities, however, because they were without fixed domicile or, more exactly, because they took for their own uses nooks and crannies not charted on the official plan of the city.

No outsider, especially years after the fact, has the right to romanticize the clochards as wanderers who moved along the river to find some place or rhythm for their lives. But they were what one least expects to find in the center of a city. My view from the river evokes them as travelers—for that word can translate a certain sense of *sans domicile fixe*— no longer visible from a *bateau-mouche* but still part of the culture of the place. A sentimental education should, among other ends, make one wonder what home can mean when it becomes a place of memory rather than a literal habitation. If home is somewhere to be shaped and reshaped through the circumstances and inventions of later experience, then it can become a pilgrimage site: a place where one goes with a sense of piety and a need to cycle back to origins. Home as habitation and as pilgrimage site must stand beside each other: my Paris next to my Buffalo. The value of crossing an inland sea, of traveling, lies partly in the way it redeems home by making it seem strange.

CHAPTER 3

Openlands: Oklahoma

Maps of the contiguous United States resemble a jigsaw puzzle put together from the outside edges in until all of the pieces are used except one. That piece looks like none of the others and barely fits the space in the center. Oklahoma.

No single route like a river running through it guides you to an understanding of this place. Schoolbooks say Oklahoma is not part of the South or the West or the Midwest, Southwest, or anywhere else: it is simply itself. Linguists interested in American regional dialects hardly know what to do with Oklahoma, so most ignore it because it fits none of their schemes. The closest I ever heard anyone get to locating the place was a remark made by a female friend born in Tulsa that women in Oklahoma think they live in the South and men think they live in the West. That would account for their dress when they go out for dinner most anywhere in the state: the women in make-up, hair, and clothes too ornate for the occasion; the men in pressed jeans, simple shirts, with a touch of the dandy in silver belt-buckle or handmade ostrich-skin boots.

If there is no single line to follow, nor any fixed center around which to make the place turn, that may be because Oklahoma bears the geographical burden of stretching some 475 miles along its straight northern border from the pine hills and shaded valleys of the east to the sage grass and sun-bleached mesas of the West. How do you resolve a place that, heading west, begins in Arkansas and ends in New Mexico? From south to north the transition is easier; cattle and then railroads were run between Texas and Kansas for years before the place was called Oklahoma. The continuity of this south-north axis, of cattle and oil, extends through the Great Plains beyond the Canadian border.

The myths of Oklahoma do not yield narratives of settlement but instead evoke again and again paths of migration. If, as Wallace Stevens writes, "a mythology reflects its region," then that of Oklahoma reflects a long-time pattern of coming and going across the land. The idea of home figures in this mythology, but as the place abandoned or the place desired, as a site of the past or of the future. Those caught among these stories rarely find a sense of home in this setting. There are ancestral memories, but they too follow routes of migration rather than a fixed line of settled generations. Somewhere at the heart of these ancestral stories is a moment of dispossession or dislocation. Even the tumbleweed that blows across the openlands in the fall is an immigrant, the fruit of a Russian thistle.

In the American imagination, Oklahoma came into being with the Land Run of 1889 and was depopulated by the Dust Bowl exodus of the 1930s. From the Sooners' covered wagons to the Okies' clapped-out jalopies was one long generation in American life; it went from the end of the frontier to the moment when America started its tilt into California. This long generation reads at first like failure:

entry into a promised land that could be inhospitable in its heat and drought, backbreaking in its clay and sand soils, peripheral to American life though almost at its geographical center. But whether this was a failure unique to the region or, more intriguingly, a repetition of American frontier experience beyond its nineteenth-century terminus—that is, beyond the prairie schooner to the Model T—one fact remains: all of these migration stories converge to form the mythology of the region.

This mythology lies beneath the thin layer of Anglo history in Oklahoma, and reveals itself through the experience of very different cultures. In the late nineteenth century, former slaves from the Old South moved to the Indian Territory in the hope of creating a black state; they were sometimes known, in an allusion to the great biblical myth about moving toward freedom, as "exodusters." Their towns remain scattered about the state but their history remains submerged and does not appear in the authorized version of the place. Only Ralph Ellison and Toni Morrison have told the stories of the old black towns of Oklahoma.

The origin myth of the Kiowa as recounted by N. Scott Momaday in *The Way to Rainy Mountain* (1969) tells of their journey to the prairie-born mountains of western Oklahoma in the late seventeenth century before the time of contact with Europeans: "The great adventure of the Kiowas was a going forth into the heart of the continent. They began a long migration from the headwaters of the Yellowstone River eastward to the Black Hills and south to the Wichita Mountains. . . . In the course of that long migration they had come of age as a people. They had conceived a good idea of themselves; they had dared to imagine and determine who they were." For Momaday this memory of migration has become a sustaining myth to be told both as

75

personal account in *The Way to Rainy Mountain* and as fiction in *House Made of Dawn* (1968). Regardless of the genre, he chose to tell this story as an emigrant looking back at Oklahoma from points further west.

Most tribal nations in Oklahoma have a different origin story, one that finds no redeeming vision of the past but instead struggles to remember the brute, imposed facts of experience. The forced resettlement in the 1830s of the Five Civilized Tribes—Cherokee, Creek, Choctaw, Chickasaw, and Seminole—from their homes in the southeastern states to Indian Territory bears a simple but evocative title that, translated from the Cherokee, means "The Road Where the People Cried" or, in the standard phrasing, "The Trail of Tears." As the Oklahoma historian Angie Debo has said of this horror: "Whether they entered upon their hopeless journey with heartbroken submission or were driven as sullen, desperate captives in chains, their suffering on the 'Trail of Tears' forms the most tragic episode in American history." Other native peoples were to be forced down similar trails during the rest of the century until Oklahoma would come to have more than fifty tribal nations, the most of any state in the union.

Other stories of Oklahoma migration have no telling phrase to fix them in memory because they concern individual rather than collective experience. Perhaps the most recurrent tells of those who came to Oklahoma as the price of oil and gas rose and then left as it fell. In the mid-1980s when that oil boom failed, apartment complexes across the state were abandoned half-built because prospective tenants left to find work elsewhere. These building sites seemed all the more desolate for being abruptly left to the elements: roughed-out 2x4 frames, sheathing blown loose from the sides, piles of gravel overgrown with weeds. It all seemed to have happened overnight, as if the crew left one afternoon at quitting time and never came back. Those who live on the boom-and-bust cycles of oil and gas, and on the crap-shoot of wheat and cotton prices set by brokers in distant cities, develop an internal rhythm that matches and even celebrates this economy of wild prosperity and wrenching poverty. In Woody Guthrie's words, "The religion of the oil fields, guys said, was to get all you can, and spend all you can as quick as you can, and then end up in the can." Nothing is forever, things come and go, grow up poor/live rich/die poor in this economy, move from place to place, follow the path of migration.

When Franz Kafka wrote his grim fantasia on life in the new world, *Amerika* (finished in 1914), he invented an amorphous but enormously benevolent organization to stand as a counterweight to rapacious American capitalism. This invention was Kafka's way to maintain that utopian possibility of a new life that has long been America's hope for Europe. Kafka, who never traveled far beyond *Mittel Europa* and certainly never crossed the Atlantic, called this organization with surprising insight the "Nature Theatre of Oklahama" (though he misspelled it). Kafka knew Oklahoma from reading the romantic westerns of Karl May, Germany's Zane Grey, and was responding to its lure as idealized, boundless space untroubled by the border disputes of Middle Europe on the brink of World War I. As far away as Prague he heard the draw of migration in the name Oklahoma. He was, however, sufficiently shrewd not to offer any description of the place. Oklahoma remained a name for Kafka, no less compelling for being misspelled.

Such has been the fate of Oklahoma as a subject. With its burden of possibility, it becomes a place of unrealizable idealization that evades precise or even evocative description. Washington Irving set the pattern. The territory that would later become Oklahoma drew Irving on his return to the United States in 1832 after seventeen years of living in Europe. During this time abroad he cultivated his reputation by writing to Americans of the old, mysterious civilizations of Europe, most famously of the Moorish glamour of the Alhambra. Yet within a few months of his return he was camping and sharing tall tales about hunting buffalo and grizzlies with a ragged band of irregular frontier soldiers amid the post oak and blackjack of the Cross Timbers in central Oklahoma. He went to the territory, he explains, because as he landed in the United States "the saddening conviction stole over my heart that I was a stranger in my own home!" For the émigré writer this is the classic moment of rediscovering what it means to be a native. That was the draw for Irving: "In the often vaunted regions of the Far West, several hundred miles beyond the Mississippi, extends a vast tract of uninhabited country, where there is neither to be seen the log house of the white man, nor the wigwam of the Indian." To be in a place before settlement, before it is corrupted by history and so demands the sophisticated responses of an Alhambra, that is the ultimate traveler's pastoral. It is also pure invention, for Irving could describe the territory as "uninhabited" only by seeing it as the hunting grounds of "the nomads of the prairies" such as the Comanche and the Pawnee. He remained European in being unable to comprehend that the nomad belongs to the land as truly as does the householder.

Irving's *Tour on the Prairies* is most interesting because its author never knew quite what to do with Oklahoma: to write a soberly detailed account of its peoples and landscapes; to romance it into a gaudy fiction à la James Fenimore Cooper; to throw himself into a new region and shed his European veneer. But amid these possibilities, Irving did discover what it means to go home by being unsettled in Oklahoma, by traveling to a place where he had never been before. Yet what made him think that he would find anything in Oklahoma that would make him less a stranger in his own home?

Irving was not the last to find himself struggling with the elusiveness of Oklahoma. Ian Frazier in his *Great Plains* (1989) passes through the Panhandle of Oklahoma on his way north from Texas but otherwise ignores the state. His reasons for doing so may be deduced from a remark he makes about his terrain as a writer: "Today you hear of people my age being urban pioneers in some neglected neighborhood, or moving to the suburbs, or moving to Northern California or Washington or northwest Montana, like me. You never hear of us moving to the Great Plains." *Great Plains* can be read, perhaps a bit unfairly, as yet another book by an easterner who passed uncomprehendingly through the middle of America, that region that cartographers once labeled literally, and thus inaccurately, as the Great American Desert. The region remains metaphorically, and far more accurately, a desert to those of Frazier's generation who moved to Washington or northern California or even northwestern Montana. It seems almost too neat a measure of Oklahoma's place in the contemporary American imagination that it could not compel mention in Frazier's book on the plains. For if not there, then where?

Another and more literal omission also came in 1989, the centenary of the great Land Run into the state, when Rand McNally published a *Photographic World Atlas* that lacked maps for three states, including Oklahoma. The governor of the state suggested that travelers needed no map to find Oklahoma because "it lies at the crossroads of America."

The metaphor may be more cruelly true than he intended, for in Oklahoma crossroads are places you pass through rather than where you settle. Or, as John Steinbeck said, Route 66 out of Oklahoma was "the mother road, the road of flight."

My telling of Oklahoma begins with its stories because they were my introduction to the place. I knew for a year before it happened that I would move there, and I spent much of that time reading Oklahoma from a studio apartment on the Upper West Side of Manhattan. As I read Steinbeck, Momaday, the standard histories, I found so many different accounts of migration that I could not locate the place in its stories. When I told people in the mid-1980s that I was moving to Norman to teach at the University of Oklahoma, I encountered a kind of perplexed incredulity. The two aging Jewish men who owned the stationery store I frequented looked at me, after hearing where I was going, as if I were heading to the Siberia of the czars—by no means a gulag, but a place of depressing exile. That the Puerto Rican deliverymen at the store raved about the university's football team strengthened their bosses' suspicions about Oklahoma.

I don't believe I ever told anyone—at least I hope I didn't—that I was going to Oklahoma to discover what it meant to be an American. Partly this was because I was willing to wager that Buffalo and New York City, places in my blood, were as much a part of America as Oklahoma or anywhere else west of the Mississippi. Partly it was because I resisted the vision of Oklahoma as the heart of the American darkness that, too kind to say so openly, my family and friends thought it was. And, finally, I knew that the pity of others was no way to look at a place.

During the five years I lived in Oklahoma, from 1986 to 1991, I traveled the state with friends who knew the terrain and its residents with a loving, if exacting, familiarity. I listened to the people I met and especially to my students who carried themselves with a complex understanding of what it meant to be an Oklahoman in the American landscape. I found myself remembering their turns of phrase, their metaphors, their cultural references as a way of understanding the place. As we talked about the history of the English language or linguistic theory or medieval literature they would tell, perhaps unconsciously but evocatively, their stories of the place. They spoke of ancestors who had made the Land Run, or of relatives who had emigrated to California, or of their own mixed blood. I also wrote, as a medievalist, a book called *Migration and Mythmaking in Anglo-Saxon England*. I had hoped, perhaps unconsciously, that some distance of time and place would illuminate the problems of cultural identity and geographical situation I encountered in Oklahoma.

I learned that not all of the necessary stories of the place are written or read. Some, at least, exist in more hidden forms that resist interpretation by outsiders. Oklahoma came to seem in my mind a land of unlikeliness, a place where you could routinely order quail and grits for brunch in an Oklahoma City grill or glimpse llamas, ostriches, and cattle grazing together in the western part of the state. Much as Oklahomans disliked her for writing *Cimarron* (1930), Edna Ferber knew the place when she observed: "Anything can have happened in Oklahoma. Practically everything has."

As you drive across the Oklahoma landscape on Friday evenings in the fall, you pass through long stretches of darkness interrupted by eerily quiet towns. They do not seem abandoned but instead depopulated, as if swept by some plague. Then as you look across the distance you will see, like prairie campfires lit to draw in travelers, circles of light under which the great ritual of the place is enacted. Like others who live in the underpopulated American west, in states too vast to have a compelling center of gravity, Oklahomans locate a sense of community in the football teams of their high schools and colleges. And, yes, in states other than Oklahoma, TV newcasts open with reports of high school seniors who have signed letters-of-intent to play football that coming fall at the state university. Only in Oklahoma, however, does football correspond so radically to the history of the place. For football distinguishes itself from baseball by being a sport played back and forth across a field, and from all other sports played back and forth, like basketball or hockey, by using the violent conquest of territory—measured in 10-yard increments rather than the 160-acre homesteads of the frontier—as the principle of victory. To score a touchdown is to make a landrun.

In Oklahoma the obsession with football belongs deep within the mythic life of the place. This may be denied or forgotten or never articulated by the 75,000 and more at Owen Field in Norman on a Saturday afternoon, but history forces itself on those who struggle to live outside of it. For when the University of Oklahoma Sooners score a touchdown, which occurred with frightening regularity during the seasons I lived in the state, the winning of territory was celebrated by the appearance of the Sooner Schooner and the firing of shotguns. The Schooner is a replica covered wagon pulled by two ponies: Boomer, named for those who promoted or "boomed" the opening of Indian Territory to Anglo homesteaders; and Sooner, named for those who jumped the gun too soon before the authorized opening of the region to Anglo settlement that began with the Land Run of 1889. Tracing one's lineage back to those who made the Land Run of '89 is the Oklahoma equivalent of New Englanders claiming descent from the *Mayflower*. Or, as a friend wrote to me in 1992 after watching the Oklahoma Sooners obliterate the Arkansas State Indians 61–0, she had seen the history of the territory reenacted on a Saturday afternoon.

That little covered wagon and its ponies may seem no more than a display of frontier kitsch redeemed, if at all, by the good spirits of the participants. Yet that such a display occurs at the largest of all public gatherings in the state— at a football game attended by a crowd more populous than all but the four or five cities in Oklahoma—shows that it does serve as the public history of the place. On the Monday after playing football against the University of Texas, on the day when the rest of America marks Columbus Day, the University of Oklahoma used to cancel classes for "Texas Weekend" to celebrate this myth for the discovery of the place. 1889, not 1492, becomes the year to commemorate.

There are very few stories of life as it has been lived on the southern plains in Oklahoma, an ecosystem so fragile that some scientists have proposed it be turned back to the prairie grasses and wandering animals of its pastoral era. There are moments or, more precisely, places where one can feel that these scientists are not utterly absurd to urge that history be reversed and the land be taken back from wheat growing and stock raising. Travel through lost towns like Gotebo and Cyril, where storefronts and refineries stand vacant to the rain and dust, and you will see that this reversion has already begun its own seemingly inexorable course.

By setting much of Oklahoma aside as Indian Territory, as a new homeland for tribal nations from the 1830s on,

Anglos had hoped to assuage their sins as Indian-killers. When the map of the United States seemed to be full and the Anglo hunger for land remained unsatisfied, the treaties with tribal nations were broken and migratory land-runs from 1889 to 1893 were organized by the federal government. A generation later, in the 1930s, Angie Debo studied how lands granted by treaty to the Five Civilized Tribes were stolen by Anglo land speculators. Debo's sympathies may be judged by the twist her title puts on the treaty phrase for designating eternal duration: "as long as the waters run and the sun shall shine" becomes *And Still the Waters Run: The Betrayal of the Five Civilized Tribes*. Debo submitted her manuscript to the University of Oklahoma Press but withdrew it after the powerful land interests she named threatened to close down the press if it published her exposé. To its credit, Princeton University Press released *And Still the Waters Run* in 1940. The University of Oklahoma Press waited until 1984 to republish it. There are so few stories by Anglos about living in Oklahoma because they have no clear title to the land, either as settlers or nomads.

Of all the stories associated with the state, Rodgers and Hammerstein's musical *Oklahoma!* (1943) is the closest to being a narrative of settlement. Drawing heavily on the play *Green Grow the Lilacs* (1931) by Oklahoma-born Lynn Riggs, *Oklahoma!* has some claim to being the story of the place. It has given the state its official song, surely the best in the nation, and a lyric for expressing pride in the place: "We know we belong to the land / And the land we belong to is grand." But beyond the ceaseless playing of "Oklahoma" before football games and other civic occasions, the musical has little connection to the history of the state. It is plains pastoral, featuring a fancy surrey and a box-supper to raise money for a new school; it strips the past of its violence, its struggles with the elements, its murderous theft of land from the Indians. It simplifies history in order to celebrate the transition from raising cattle to growing grain, from the unsettled migratory life to the fixed agricultural routine. As Curly puts it in *Green Grow the Lilacs*: "Oh, things is changin' right and left! Buy up mowin' machines, cut down the prairies! Shoe yer horses, drag them plows under the sod!" In 1943, Rodgers and Hammerstein knew that America wanted a romance of fertile corn and tender love to sustain it through the war years. Yet again, Oklahoma had to bear the weight of outsiders' idealizing.

In a transient land rich with stories of migration, history lies not in what is preserved artificially, such as the old barracks at Fort Sill where Geronimo and other Indian leaders of the 1890s were imprisoned, but in the abandoned farmhouses throughout the state that survive, windowless, to the wind and sun. These remains memorialize those who lived on the edge and could not weather the harsh life of Oklahoma. They were built to shelter those who came with visions of the promised land and then were either "tractored off," in Steinbeck's metaphor for the fate of sharecroppers and small farmers of the thirties, or were, in a hard time, simply forgotten. Around these abandoned farmsteads one typically finds a stand of trees planted when the house was built and that now marks it as the site of earlier settlement. These small groves break the flow of grain or cotton sweeping along to the horizon. The land of those who once lived in these houses has often been joined to the spreads of more successful neighbors, though success here may simply have meant having a bit more water. Abandoned farmhouses appear everywhere in the American landscape, but those in Oklahoma have entered the national imagination through the enduring black-and-white images of the Dust Bowl

taken by Arthur Rothstein and the other Farm Security
Agency photographers of the late thirties.

So it is with towns like the fabled Gotebo of southwest
Oklahoma, the place that signifies "the middle of nowhere"
or "the back of beyond" to central Oklahomans. Gotebo has
a row of what were once fine stone-built stores that displayed a solid prosperity and testified to their builders' faith
in the future. Now the storefronts have collapsed, the roofs
cannot keep out the rain, and the stores are filled with rusting junk. A town built for the long haul collapsed within a
generation or two. It seems an act of mercy that today the
state highway skirts the town and leads drivers past newly
built gas stations and convenience stores. All that indicates
the town's center from the highway is a sign pointing with
unconsciously cruel irony to the "Business District" of Gotebo. I doubt one could spend a dollar there.

The evidence of busted dreams lies along the sides of
roads leading into and out of Oklahoma. Only the land and
the minerals that lie beneath its surface have enduring
value. Buildings are abandoned as if without substantial
being, some within a few years of being built, others before
completion because the money ran out or the market dried
up or someone just moved on. The roadside ruins of old
farms, tiny hamlets collapsing around the church and filling
station, shattered main streets in small towns all speak of
lives that didn't work out in a place that couldn't hold its
people. Ian Frazier puts it beautifully: "You can find all kinds
of ruins on the Great Plains; in dry regions, things last a
long time."

I photographed empty houses bleached to silver-gray by
the sun; standing on the edge of enormous fields, they were
quietly moving in their mute isolation. I thought they might
yield their stories to the camera. Through the viewfinder I

saw the farmsteads before me but also the great photographs from the 1930s. The images did not correspond exactly, nor did I try to find the places where the originals were taken. I wanted instead to balance the present site and the remembered photograph and thus create a stereopticon image of the scene. As I traveled with friends along Highway 3 into the Panhandle, we found ourselves calling each of these sites "the old homestead." It was the nervous joke of those unsettled by the remains of suffering, by the thought that too much of the American past is a lost house along a road leading westward.

No one will ever restore any of the houses along Highway 3. That kind of preservation belongs instead to a site like Blue Hawks Peak, the elaborate ranch belonging to "Pawnee Bill" (Major Gordon W. Lillie) who was competitor and friend to Buffalo Bill during the era of the great Wild West shows. The mansion house was built in 1910 at a cost of $100,000. From the outside it harmonizes with the terrain and vernacular architecture of Oklahoma; made of roughly dressed fieldstone and timber it stands two stories high with a steeply gabled roof and a long view across the landscape. Everything proclaims it to be the house of the local grandee. Inside, only the fine Navajo rugs suggest that the house is in the West. Otherwise, it seems the home of a wealthy easterner with strictly conventional tastes: Steinway grand piano in the living room, Philippine mahogany woodwork throughout the downstairs, a Tiffany silver tea service in the dining room, Chinese ceramic tiles in the bathrooms, French chandeliers throughout, a barber chair in Pawnee Bill's dressing room. Like all of the old western showmen, he was more dandy than cowboy. The disjunction between outside and inside at Pawnee Bill's dream house seems emblematic of the place and time; the newness of Anglo settlement allowed this sort of eccentricity to flourish—in fact, demanded it to counter the fear of losing one's place on the land. The depth of Anglo settlement in Oklahoma is so shallow that local historical societies seem determined to put a plaque on almost anything that has lasted the years. But the restored houses and forts seem less accurate as a register of time and its passing than do towns like Gotebo.

Touring Pawnee Bill's house, I imagined Henry James visiting him and writing about it for *The American Scene*. As a master of American ambivalence, James would have caught perfectly that need to blend into the landscape and also the desire to scandalize the neighbors with one's sophistication. James, better than anyone in America at the time, would have understood Pawnee Bill as he lived out his life of European refinement in a small county seat in northeastern Oklahoma. He would have measured to the last the psychic cost of living such a life. He might also have predicted that the place would be preserved as a stage set to glorify for later generations this self-made showman of the Indian Territory.

The guide who led us around the house explained that when Pawnee Bill got out of the Wild West business, he retired to his ranch and, as lord of the manor, oversaw what was then the largest private herd of buffalo in the world. But the guide didn't tell us where Bill went for a smoke or a drink with the ranchhands when all that elegance became too burdensome and he wanted to retell the old stories about leading a band of settlers in the Run of '89.

The unrestored history of Oklahoma lies in farms and town centers that ebb away with each passing year, in the grown-over cuts where railroads once ran and in the ruts etched on the prairie from the trails followed by cattle drovers north or homesteaders west. The real historical evidence, the physical remains speak quietly of people who came and went, and that pattern shapes the stories about Oklahoma.

The fugitive past of Oklahoma struck most vividly at the Mount Olivet Cemetery in Hugo, a town in the southeast of the state just above the Texas border. The town came into being when two railway lines—one north-south, the other east-west—crossed and gave access to all points on the map. In 1901, the wife of the railroad's right-of-way agent named the town after her favorite novelist. Its location soon made it the winter base for two traveling circuses. Over time Hugo became home for the circus people, and they chose to be buried together there in a section of the cemetery called Showman's Rest. Their stones have all the gaudy beauty and sentimentaliy that once lured kids to join the circus. Today, they draw visitors to the cemetery: a large gray granite memorial with images of a trumpeting elephant and a circus tent stands as A TRIBUTE TO ALL SHOWMEN UNDER GOD'S BIG TOP; a multicolored stone version of a circus wagon wheel reads THERE'S NOTHING LEFT BUT EMPTY POPCORN SACKS AND WAGON TRACKS—THE CIRCUS IS GONE; a stone remembering a husband and wife who ran concession stands testifies WE HAD THE GOOD LIFE BUT THE SEASON ENDED.

In that cemetery, beyond the graves of the circus people and a regional celebrity, Freckles Brown the Cowboy, beyond where visitors go, there is a small section filled with flat headstones of the sort that usually mark the graves of old soldiers. When I first saw this section all of the stones had small white crosses except for one that had a small white Star of David. There was something so utterly arresting about it that I got out of the car to read the stone: "Morris Goldfeder, 1st SGT. U. S. Army, World War I, 1894–1977."

89

What was that one Jew doing in Mount Olivet Cemetery in Hugo, Oklahoma, so far from any of his *landsleit*?

Perhaps, like other migrant Jews who came to Oklahoma in the early days, he started off as a peddler and then ran the local general store. Did he, like Sol Levy, the Alsatian Jew who goes from peddler to mercantile magnate in *Cimarron*, encounter an increasingly virulent anti-Semitism as the state became more settled? How, if he read that novel, would he have responded to Sol Levy's description of his fellow settlers in the Land Run of '89: "Those barbarians! My ancestors were studying the Talmud and writing the laws the civilized world now lives by when theirs were swinging from tree to tree." This was my surmise about Morris Goldfeder, my attempt to make his wandering part of the fugitive nature of the place. Then I read his obituary and heard stories about him. Morris Goldfeder settled in Hugo in 1911 and in fact did run a store there for many years. He was remembered for his acts of charity to those in need; his Christian neighbors spoke of him as a "saint" because he was unobtrusively generous and kind. Jews would have understood him as something less elevated but rarer, a *mensh*.

It seemed right that the migratory pattern of this Bible-belt state should be represented by the grave of a Jewish soldier in a town named for a French romantic novelist. It seemed so utterly unlikely and thus perfect. The people of the place were never resident long enough to leach the unlikeliness out of them. A few days before I left Oklahoma in 1991, I drove the 140 miles or so from Norman to Hugo because I wanted to visit the cemetery again and remember this grave that had become my private story of the place. I saw from a distance, as I knew I would, the cluster of small white crosses above the flat headstones. This time no Star of David appeared among them. Was it looted as a curiosity, removed as inappropriate for a Christian cemetery, or simply being repaired? All I could know was that I would not have stopped to look at this grave if I had first visited the cemetery that day, and thus would have felt all the more transient during my five years in Oklahoma. That stone mattered to me. It spoke of diaspora as a human condition. Here, in the middle of the forty-eight states, one had no choice but to tell the oldest of all travel stories, that of searching for home.

There are other forms of transience, of rootlessness, of forgetting the past because the essential line of human continuity, and thus of oral transmission, has been broken. If a place is as much its stories as its terrain, then its identity becomes diminished as stories are suppressed by those who think them dangerous or are lost because those who could tell them have moved on or died off. To trace if the stories still circulated, I would tell my students at the university that Oklahoma was once alive with radical fervor, that Eugene V. Debs and the Socialist Party got some 42,000 votes (16.6 percent of the state total) in the presidential election of 1912; that many hundreds of armed farmers rose against World War I conscription during the Green Corn Rebellion of August 1917; that my father as a young man in the Bronx of the 1930s eagerly read socialist publications from Oklahoma. I would tell them about the summer encampments in towns like Hugo where socialists would gather for a week, as if it were a religious revival, to hear their great speakers: Debs, Caroline Low, and Oscar Ameringer, the Oklahoma native whose autobiography, *If You Don't Weaken*, offers a vivid account of those years. I would recommend that they read James R. Green's remarkable *Grass-Roots Socialism*, which proved against the conventional pieties that radicalism had once run deep in Oklahoma.

These stories no longer circulated in a state where populism had come to mean little more than a reactionary protest against taxes or big government and where, in 1991, someone could still think it worthwhile to pay for a huge billboard along an interstate highway to proclaim in bold black letters against a white background: ALL SOCIALISM IS BAD! My students were fascinated by these stories because they had never heard them before or had at most been told in passing that some farmers in the state flirted briefly with socialism before quickly returning to their senses. In the end, though, they could not comprehend these stories; they could not, in the most literal sense, locate a radical politics in the state of Oklahoma. The old radicals were long dead and their lives had been brutally excised from approved schoolbooks. These stories of the place are gone.

Instead of a communal, socialist politics there circulates in the state a flourishing countermyth of rugged individualism: great men are those who take for themselves a fortune from the earth in minerals, crops, ranching. Or they are those who live independent of institutional restraints: cowboys and wild-cat oilmen, political demagogues and television evangelists. What Steinbeck understood best in *The Grapes of Wrath* was that Tom Joad's vision of solidarity came too late, in the migrant camps of California after he and his fellow Okies had already been broken by emigration.

My first sight of the state was from a jet coming in to land at Will Rogers Airport in Oklahoma City; at perhaps a thousand feet, the clouds that had blocked the view broke apart and the land appeared below with its slightly rolling waves ironed dead level by the perspective. All the jokes about the flatness of Oklahoma—start a bowling ball in one county and watch it roll through the next four or five—seemed true.

But as you learn to look at the landscape of Oklahoma from the air, you see the fresh green of young wheat, the dusty white of harvest cotton, section roads cut at relentless right angles to each other, occasional circles of lush growth watered by massive rotating sprinklers. The land below is laid out by some inhuman geometry impeded only by rock and water. As you fly in late in the day, the setting sun reflects thousands of ponds and pools scattered across the prairie. The land hoards water in even the smallest of depressions, hardly noticeable at ground level.

By learning the terrain of a new place, you can feel yourself settle in. The prairie, at a quick glance from a plane, is like the sea from the same vantage: featureless, lifeless, undifferentiated. At level, though, both take on a complexity and gradation that are continually surprising as you watch them. On the prairie, slow rises and crumbling slopes along the flanks of creekbeds provide shelter from the ceaseless wind that blows from the west. Cattle drift toward this shelter as naturally as they drift toward water. The undulating prairie frequently erupts into hills, mesas, stony outcrops, high cornices of rimrock along the horizon line that frame the landscape into patterns for viewing. Travelers who complain about the flat monotony of Oklahoma as they head west on I-40 from the center of the state toward the Texas line have the foreshortened vision of city dwellers. Where the land lies ironed flat you must learn to look up at a covering sky that becomes all the more limitless as you relinquish the desire for visible landmarks or measures of human scale. The earth in Oklahoma flows imperceptibly, though sometimes violently, into the sky. And that sky is always alive with light: the jewel blue of a cloudless day, the grayish green that comes before a storm. The light in

Oklahoma always reminds you that you are in one of the great openlands of the world.

The views in Oklahoma are not the famous ones you travel hours to see only to glance at because they are so familiar. The place gives up its views sparingly, even grudgingly, and then only to those who find beauty in a stand of cottonwood and willow along a stream or in the gentle rise of the land as it runs out the miles. The drama of the scene rests in the flow between land and sky. Oklahomans watch the sky with the knowing respect of ocean sailors. They look up at it regularly during the day, and describe it with a quiet gesture or laconic phrase. If each place has a defining disaster, a phenomenon that makes for nightmares, Oklahoma's is the tornado because it comes suddenly from the sky and follows no predictable path. Experienced tornado-watchers all say that you can't know when the funnel will veer away or touch down. It's transitory, destructive, a product of topography. Oklahomans display a certain nonchalance about tornadoes; they mockingly call storm cellars "fraidy holes" and ignore warning sirens. Yet that nonchalance masks a deep respect that one hears not in comments about tornadoes in general but rather in the stories told about particular tornadoes and their aftermath in towns across the state. People speak with fascination about a school bus being lifted up and then dropped four or five miles away or—and here voices go from awestruck to mystical—of the houses that suffered no damage because the tornado only sliced down one side of Main Street.

During the spring, the state becomes "Tornado Alley" and the openness of the land takes on a new menace. Drivers watch the sky for funnel clouds and the bar-ditch along the edge of the road for shelter. When you live in a place that seems to provide no protection at moments of danger, you learn to look at the world differently. The terrain of Oklahoma teaches you that all is open to view precisely because nothing can be kept hidden or secret. It teaches you how to approach the people who live in it. Their manner when you meet them has a certain wary openness about it that is usually accompanied in women by a smile. Conversation about certain topics is possible: the weather is always safe and sometimes becomes a metaphor for more painful subjects; football during the season is inevitable, though it pays to be careful about respecting fan loyalties.

But just as the terrain shows itself to be graded and varied rather than merely flat, so the people prove at times silent and private. Despite their initial openness, they are careful to keep away from certain topics. For all of the various religious faiths in the state, Oklahomans are sensitive about revealing, to use a phrase of the place, their "church home." This reserve is especially present when they speak with outsiders who are likely, they have learned, to think of them as barefoot, snake-handling holy rollers who speak in tongues at revival meetings held in tents late at night as the kids sleep in the back of the pickup and the teenagers drift off for their own communion. When neighbors or students felt free to talk about religion with me, I took it as a sign of acceptance.

To speak of a "church home" rather than a denomination is most characteristic of Baptists, Church of Christ, or Pentecostals like Assembly of God or Nazarene; that is, of those who belong to the autonomous churches that shape the religious cast of the state. Those who cultivate a sense of church hierarchy and thus a connection beyond the borders of the state—Presbyterians, Methodists, or Episcopalians—are not likely to use the term. Those who do use it suggest thereby that beyond the path of literal migration there is a spiritual migration in the place; this sense that home can be found in a religious community utterly unique to itself and without any other congregation corresponds to the historical circumstances of those who came to the state. Roadside churches with names like Living Water Tabernacle or Highway Tabernacle are communities that have come together around a shared, though not necessarily doctrinal or denominational, reading of Scripture. For those who must dig deep to root themselves into the land, the making of a spiritual home becomes an anchor against the flow of migration.

The church home offers some intimacy, some human contact in the far distant spaces that otherwise enforce separation and isolation. For, above all else, "loneliness is an aspect of the land," as Momaday says, and thus "all things in the plain are isolate." As a consequence, the idea of not belonging to groups built around churches, sports teams, service clubs, and the like comes to seem ominous. One can live apart from mainstream culture in the openlands but doing so requires a vantage point that enables one to look around and set oneself within the landscape. The long unobstructed views of Oklahoma can at times create a false sense of knowledge about the surrounding world. Surprises seem impossible when the horizon line is so clearly distant. Hill people, I imagine, never develop this sense of security but instead cultivate a necessary suspicion because they have such short vistas. One lives differently where there are no sharp curves or steep grades in the road but only the platted right-angles of the prairie. Looking at Australia, Alan Moorehead captures a quality of the landscape that seems to explain life in all of the great continental openlands: "claustrophobia in the midst of such an infinity of space."

Driving along the highway from Oklahoma City into the southwest corner of the state, into a landscape that matches the mind's-eye view of Oklahoma, you encounter a range of old, rounded mountains that seem to have been heaved up, without foothills or any preparatory rise, from the level of the prairie. The Wichita Mountains are now within the borders of a federal wildlife refuge that shelters buffalo, longhorn cattle, elk, as well as eagles and, when the rain does not flood them out, a colony or two of prairie dogs. The buffalo descend from those shipped out by rail from the Bronx Zoo in 1905 because almost none were left roaming the plains. As you leave the highway at the Medicine Park exit to pick up the state road to the refuge, you pass a small cluster of new buildings that serve as the Comanche Tribal Complex.

The sign for this complex marks a shift in the terrain from mapped route to spiritual landscape. I once drove two French writers to see the Wichitas, and they, having never met in France, spent an hour and a half in the backseat talking happily of mutual friends in the literary world as we drove from Norman. As the car slowed for the exit, one of them looked out the window, saw the sign, and exclaimed "Co-manch!" Then they knew themselves to be out of France. They were in a landscape that figured Oklahoma to them: jagged hills broken by slabs of red granite, herds of buffalo and elk, the light brown grasses of the winter prairie. They looked for cowboys. Being writers, they debated what the French word for elk might be; they knew *bison* for buffalo. When we stepped out of the car to look at a clump of buffalo ranged up a hillside, the Frenchmen looked instead with fascination at a road-kill that was, one of them said, a cross between reptile and mammal. It was an armadillo, though none of us knew that *tatou* was its French name. I explained that the folklore of the place had it that no one ever saw a live armadillo; they were only found dead along the roadside.

97

From the prairie floor to the top of the Wichita Mountain outcrops is relatively little if measured as a vertical rise; the tallest, Mount Scott, is only 2,464 feet high but it gives a long vista from its summit. One of the triumphs of WPA construction allows you to drive to the top of Mount Scott; as you circle your way up the mountain, you see with a kind of omniscience the entire landscape around you. When you circle your way around the mountain and then return to the same view, but at several hundred feet above your last glimpse of it, you sense the landscape continually shifting and complicating itself. From the top, where the weather dislocates you by being intensely hotter or colder than below, and where the wind always seems to find you, you first see other mountains in this small range and then numerous bodies of water, dots that resolve into buffalo or cattle, scars of old trails across the prairie. This is very near to the landscape evoked at the opening of *The Way to Rainy Mountain*: "The hardest weather in the world is there. Winter brings blizzards, hot tornadic winds arise in the spring, and in summer the prairie is an anvil's edge. The grass turns brittle and brown, and it cracks beneath your feet. There are green belts along the rivers and creeks, linear groves of hickory or pecan, willow and witch hazel." From the top of Mount Scott you can hear with concussive force the artillery being fired on the ranges of Fort Sill a few miles away.

When I took these two Frenchmen to the top of Mount Scott, I wanted them to feel rhapsodically that they were face to face with a landscape that would always be America for them. I wanted this austere scene to scar the map of places they carried with them and wrote about. As we looked at the country below, the professor from the Sorbonne turned to the novelist from Aix-la-Provence and said that this territory had all belonged to France before Napoleon sold it to

Jefferson as part of the Louisiana Purchase in 1803. The other had forgotten this fact, if he had ever known it, but it moved him to know that a thin trace of his history survived to connect him to this alien landscape. This desire to place a landscape in history seemed at first utterly French and thus incomprehensibly foreign to me. It was a moment, I thought, that defined the cultural divide between Americans and Europeans. They see history; we see landscape.

Thinking back on this brief exchange between the two Frenchmen has forced me to realize, however, that Oklahomans have at times found their landscapes too austere to face directly and thus have invented histories for them. Not surprisingly, these imposed histories connect the place not to its tribal past but rather to the Old World from where these migrants came. The most notable of these inventions is a bizarre construction in the wildlife refuge of the Wichitas that is called Holy City. It is, as its name suggests, a stage set made from native red granite where local residents perform a passion play during the Easter season. For the rest of the year, the twelve Stations of the Cross stand gauntly outlined against the blue Oklahoma sky with an otherworldly eeriness. An émigré Austrian pastor was sent in the 1920s to tend to the souls of Indians and came to feel, in what must have been a hallucination of loneliness, that the landscape of the Wichita Mountains bore an exact resemblance to that of Judea. He then built over the years a dramatic setting to take himself and his followers back to their spiritual homeland.

Another site has this same pathos of invented tradition. In the town of Heavener, not far from the Arkansas border, there is a small state park built around a runic inscription cut into a sandstone boulder that lies in a heavily wooded valley. This inscription of eight runic letters, each about

99

eight inches tall, was discovered by a local citizen in 1910. It has since been deciphered to record the presence of Vikings in the area in 1012—or at least it has by those willing to overlook its use of two different runic alphabets. To those of a more skeptical mind, this inscription seems as genuine as a graffito proclaiming "Kilroy was here!" in a mix of roman and cyrillic characters. The story of this place claims that Vikings found their way from sites in Vinland to eastern Oklahoma by a web of rivers: the St. Lawrence through the Great Lakes down the Mississippi to the Arkansas and then south a few miles by land to Heavener. Why they stopped there and turned back goes unexplained in this story. Perhaps they encountered some local monster that drove them out of this paradise.

The inscription on that boulder is a forgery, but its presence testifies eloquently to the need to leave our name or mark on the place. Against the landscape and its terrors, the traces left by precursors seem comforting and help us to locate the unlikeliness of the place. When such traces do not exist, then they must be cut into or built out of the landscape. The true history of the Heavener Runestone and of Holy City is that each was created to ease the pain of migration by evoking the past of a distant place.

In the opening frames of *The Grapes of Wrath*, Henry Fonda as Tom Joad travels from the penitentiary at McAlester down those familiar platted roads to a home that is no more, in fact, to a house abandoned and a family packing up to leave. That is one version, perhaps the best known, of this story of migration. For all of Steinbeck's errors, such as letting the dust bowl drift several hundred miles east of its actual edge to reach the Sallisaw of the Joads, he got that much right. Oklahomans have never forgiven Steinbeck in their hearts for what he did. A friend who grew up as a

Baptist in a small, southern Oklahoma town in the 1960s was told not to read his "naughty book." It suggested revival meetings were occasions for forbidden sex but worse, it told a story of dislocation that those who stayed behind could not bear to have told.

Oklahomans to this day accuse Steinbeck of mocking and reviling "Okies," of making what had been a term of pride into a slur, of having no sympathy with the common people despite his leftist politics. Perhaps there was some truth in all of this; the more than 100,000 Oklahomans who went to California in the 1930s knew that they were called Okies out of contempt and fear. As an unnamed Oklahoman returning home after being defeated by California explains to Tom Joad: "Well, Okie use' ta mean you was from Oklahoma. Now it means you're a dirty son-of-a-bitch. Okie means you're scum. Don't mean nothing itself, it's the way they say it." What must be understood is the fear that lay behind "Okie" when used by Californians and others to insult the rural poor who left Oklahoma and also Arkansas, Texas, Missouri, and the like. The word meant, finally, anyone who came from a place too hard and too poor to sustain the dream of America as a new eden. Okie came to mean those who migrated because they had been betrayed by a myth. And that was too painful a thought for those who lived in what would come to be called, after World War II, Lotus Land.

This sense that the last place to be filled in the map of the contiguous forty-eight could not sustain its mythic burden has come now, some sixty years or more after the start of the great Oklahoma migrations west, to have its reversal in the story of some old Okies who, grown prosperous through the increase in value of their bungalows in Bakersfield and elsewhere in the Central Valley of California, return to Oklahoma. The story goes that they buy a nice house on the lake and live off the rest of their capital gains. For some, California turned out to be the promised land. They survived there as Oklahomans because they transplanted their regional culture to the Central Valley in the form of Pentecostal religion, country music, a passion for football, and dialect patterns. Like so many other immigrants in America, these Oklahomans remade the world they had left behind.

These Oklahomans in California—"Califokies"—from the thirties onward followed a continual pattern of moving back and forth between the two places to do seasonal work or to visit relatives. Some went home to the prairie to die, or because it seemed better to be poor in one's native place. Oklahomans have always been, in Dan Morgan's phrase, a "drifting, mobile people." As it passes through Oklahoma, I-40 today carries many cars with California tags and more than a few of them bear signs of coming from the Oklahoma-ized regions of California, especially around Fresno. One Saturday in the fall, when the University of Southern California was playing football against the University of Oklahoma, the streets of Norman seemed full of these cars. Those who rode in them had all of the outward signs of California success and style—elegantly casual clothes and healthy suntans—but when they stopped to say hello you heard a tone in their voices that said they had come home. Their pilgrimage to Norman for that football game answers for me the question suggested by Erskine Caldwell in 1963: "When you see the scarred landscape of the dust bowl and the wind-lashed skeletons of abandoned barns and farm houses, you wonder where the people went."

If you spend a night in the Oklahoma Panhandle, you are likely to stay in Guymon, a town of slightly fewer than eight

thousand that stands at the center of the three counties—
Beaver, Texas, Cimarron—that once made up "No Man's
Land" between Texas to the south, Colorado and Kansas to
the north, New Mexico to the west, and Oklahoma to the
east. In the eastern part of the Panhandle, measureless fields
of wheat and looming grain elevators sketch out the contours of the landscape. Driving across the west of Canada,
Mark Abley thought of these elevators as "watchers of the
prairie dead." I never forgot that phrase when looking at
these Panhandle landscapes. Further west the terrain breaks
up and becomes more arid, stonier, punishingly severe until
you reach Black Mesa, the highest point in Oklahoma at
4978 feet. The land here is given over to cattle.

This is the region where they still remember the Dust
Bowl, where the photographs that belong to America's collective memory of suffering were taken. Partly because of
their history, partly because of their geography, the three
counties of the Panhandle form a region distinct in themselves; they belong to Oklahoma but in an incomplete, unsettled way. They seem to look inward, more to Guymon as
a center than to Oklahoma City. The Yellow Pages of these
counties are as likely to refer you to stores and services in
the surrounding four states as to those in Oklahoma. If you
need an abortion, for instance, you will have to call Ama-
rillo, Texas.

Few tourists visit the Panhandle, though Oklahomans
taking a shortcut to the mountains of Colorado pass through
it. I wanted to see the Panhandle, though, because people
in the center of the state would typically describe it as a
moonscape, our post-Apollo image for the uninhabitable. I
wanted a natural beauty too austere for guidebooks or cozy,
moralizing essays by nature writers. I wanted something beyond the scenic or unspoiled: I needed to see the edge of

103

nowhere. So, in the fall of 1989, in one of those periodic fits of restlessness that can only be eased by a thousand miles or so of blacktop road, I went to the Panhandle with my wife and friends.

As we drove along Highway 3 in the late October afternoon, the sun hung above the horizon line for what seemed like hours. We had been told to eat Saturday supper when we reached Guymon at a steakhouse that had the best food in town. Walking into this family restaurant, decorated with the cattle and cowboy motifs of the region, I heard a voice say in wonder: "Doctor Howe! What are you doing here?" It belonged to a student, a young woman with a fine, dreamy intelligence who'd taken a linguistics course with me. She had done well but seemed always to be thinking of elsewhere as she sat in the classroom.

I tried to tell her and the family that sat around her at a big table that the landscape had a kind of beauty in its emptiness, an elemental starkness that was not scenic and thus unnerving. I could not find the right words to answer her question. If I had known it then, I might have borrowed the title of Gretel Ehrlich's *The Solace of Open Spaces* to explain what drew me to the Panhandle. My student listened and then, as if to remind me that my visit was a weekend idyll, said with quiet finality: "But there's nothing here." At that moment I saw her parents, amiable and surprisingly young to have a daughter in college, wince as if they had taken a body blow they saw coming but could not shield themselves against. Whatever they might have thought their daughter would do once she had finished school in Norman, they knew then that she would not return to settle in Guymon. They heard in her words the old story, of coming and going, of passing through in search of somewhere to call home.

At times I would remember this exchange and feel guilty for being a part of all that drew this young woman away from Guymon and her parents. Yet that was simply my vanity, because what drove her to go wherever she went was the rhythm of the place, the same rhythm one could hear beneath her words that Saturday night in Guymon.

When I first wrote about Oklahoma after leaving there in 1991, I ended my story of the place with this visit to Guymon. I had moved on, as I predicted my student would, and I evaded my own experience by writing of hers. Perhaps I was not yet able to admit my need for the place. Perhaps I was not yet willing to set my story in a larger chronicle of migration and the openlands. All I know now was that at forty, struggling to write a eulogy for my father, I found myself remembering a visit he made to me in Oklahoma. It was a memory of unlikeliness. He had come in the fall of 1986 and we took a daytrip to the Wichita Mountains. He laughed with pleasure when I told him that the buffalo came originally from the Bronx Zoo because he had grown up near there in the 1920s and 1930s. As we sat in the November sun eating sandwiches and drinking coffee, he talked about the landscape and the way its hard vastness evoked fundamental qualities of American life for him. If he seemed out of place there in his city clothes and his New York quickness, the place itself was not alien to him.

For years it had been part of the American terrain he knew as a reader. After lunch we drove deeper into the mountains and visited Holy City. Gazing at the stage set for the Easter pageant, savoring the story of the émigré pastor who built it, smiling at our being together there of all places in the world, he turned to me and said: "It's straight out of Flannery O'Connor." I never felt closer to him than at that moment, for with that sentence he gave me a story to help me live in an alien place. Now, in memory, I see that consolation was only possible because we were alone there in a place far from home, together in a landscape made by migration.

Pilgrimage Sites: Starting from Chartres

CHARTRES

Three-quarters of the way up the cathedral's north tower, pausing to catch my breath, I looked down at the step. Over generations, pilgrims had worn a curved hollow into the stone that made the footing treacherous. So, at some point, the hollow had been cut square and a new piece set in place to make it level. The work was done neatly and the seam was barely visible, having been smoothed by the feet that walked on it. For all I could tell this was not the first patch to have been put in place. All I could know from that step was that countless others had walked here for centuries to visit the house of the Virgin Mary. What was hard to know today was if walking the 306 steps to the top of this tower could make a late twentieth-century tourist with a camera around his neck into a pilgrim.

Could such a transformation be that simple for me or anyone else in 1999? And could it be that private, that unmarked by outward ritual? This was my fifth or sixth visit to

Chartres, always arriving by train from Gare Montparnasse.
The trip between Paris and Chartres is on a suburban com-
muter line, often served by double-decker cars. A less spiritual form of transport could hardly be imagined, but that did
not matter because, as the train neared Chartres, one could
for a moment glimpse the cathedral's two towers. That was
not quite the same, but still something like, the distant view
that medieval pilgrims had as they made the slow walk
across the plain toward Chartres. After first sighting the
towers, though, they would have continued to gaze at them
for hours as they thought penitential thoughts or let their
souls dream of the Virgin's mercy.

Taking the train in and out of Chartres hardly seems like
a pilgrimage: the tired commuters, the little stations jammed
with parked automobiles, the shortness of the journey. But
if you notice that your fellow tourists on that train come
from all over the world, then the chance that this might be
a pilgrimage becomes less remote: the young Japanese couple in the seats in front of us, she with cameras and he with
a beautiful ricepaper sketchbook full of drawings of Paris
sights; the elegant older Italians talking among themselves
about the beautiful "duomo" at Chartres. The Italian word
for "cathedral" comes from their love of domes, and seemed
incongruous for Chartres because that cathedral with its two
towers seems to have invented the vertical, first as Romanesque and then again as Gothic. Yet their word was a
reminder that pilgrims by nature come from afar and speak
about a site in their own idiom of desire. There were also,
among the tourists, the two of us: both Americans, one a
novelist, the other a medievalist. Over the past twenty years
or so we had sat in the cathedral in all weathers and watched
the blue of the stained glass change with every movement
of sun and clouds, we had read aloud from Henry Adams's

Mont St. Michel and Chartres, we had discovered the old town that lay along the river below the cathedral.

If we were pilgrims, all of us on those trains to and from Chartres, then the rules of pilgrimage had changed since believers first made their way there in the twelfth century. And if the rules had changed, how then was one to define the term, one famously vague even in the Middle Ages, as every reader of Chaucer knows. And if we weren't, did that mean only those who came to the cathedral for love of the Virgin Mary and atonement for their sins could be called pilgrims?

Looking up at the cathedral as you enter Chartres by train, or as you leave at night, you see how it is balanced on the hill above the plain. Pilgrims coming from Paris and points north used to enter the city through the Porte Guillaume at the base of this hill; the gate itself was destroyed in 1944. From its site, set below on the plain, you can still look at the towers soaring upwards twice as high as they do when you approach the west facade at street level. It is about the vertical, this cathedral, and thus about the desire to enter and ascend.

Inside the cathedral at Chartres there is no set path to make visitors move through it at a decorous, efficient pace, as there is now in Paris at Notre-Dame. There, you must follow a circuit around the church because of the crowds: you enter through the south portal of the west facade and then make your way around the church counter-clockwise. The chairs that were once in the nave have been removed, leaving an inhospitable space. You cannot sit and gaze upwards. At Chartres, you can wander at will to discover the stunning ways in which space, form, and light rearrange themselves as you move through the interior. The spiritual geometry inside the cathedral continually refigures itself

111

depending on your vantage. This freedom makes Chartres feel much less like a tourist site than does Notre-Dame in Paris, for such sites are characterized by the set path and the fixed view. There, signs tell you where to stand, admire, photograph. That you are still free to choose how you will look at Chartres suggests that the visitor who returns over the years may gain something like a pilgrim's sense of the place.

At Chartres there is also the power of the stained glass. Its lure is so great that you keep looking up until you feel disoriented and your feet are not always sure of the ground. Another form of disorientation comes when, after sitting in the cathedral for an hour or so to watch the light move across the contraries of stone and glass, you go out into the impossible harshness of daylight. For the believer it must be a reminder that one cannot live easily outside the church, outside the building and the communion, without the glass and its illumination. For the nonbeliever there is a different kind of reminder: that places of human-made beauty, however inspired, can move us to disquietude and a saving confusion.

Amid all of the visitors to the cathedral, armed with their cameras and flashes, their guidebooks and strollers, the occasional old woman with a plastic bag from Monoprix will sometimes cut through the crossing from south to north transept to get out of the rain. The passage in the cathedral from transept to transept is still a route that one can take and, on the way, pay one's respects to the Virgin. That I noticed this woman's path at all shows we distinguish sacred from secular space more strictly than did the medieval residents of a cathedral town. Pilgrims in the twelfth century would sleep on the porch or in the narthex of a cathedral; it showed no disrespect to eat and rest peaceably in the house of the Virgin. Less certain of how to be in such places we move with the awkwardness of overly earnest visitors for whom the divine is not part of daily life. So then why, to press the question again, do we visit such places as Chartres? What do we get? What do we need?

Going to mass could not answer these questions, but watching others there did help me think about them. At the 6 P.M. mass on the last Thursday in August, there were about eighty people present, including some who obviously did not live in the cathedral parish. The small gathering clustered around the altar within the choir while the tourist procession circled around the apse. The truly sacred space of the cathedral, the site where the liturgy was performed, has for much of the week shrunk within the larger building. We sat back in the nave, so as not to intrude on the worshippers as I wrote in my notebook. The place at such moments has its own synesthesia: the sounds of prayer and the flash of strobes, fitful illumination amid the constant murmur of voices.

As the day closed within the cathedral on a rainy evening in late summer the glass of the windows darkened by just so much less than did the stonework that surrounds it. The colors, especially the reds, grew more vibrant before they lost the light, as do the coals of a woodfire. During the mass, an impeccably dressed woman walked through the nave toward the choir on the toes of her shoes, balancing forward so that she didn't make the usual rat-a-tat-tat of a French-woman in high heels, that rhythm that announces there is business to be done and no one should interfere. She did not join the congregation at mass, but the memory of a Catholic girlhood survived in the restraint of her manners. The acoustics of the cathedral are surprisingly good. Even from the far end of the nave the priest could be heard intoning his prayers in French. He used a sacramental, full-throated voice for prayers, and a more didactic, clipped one for the homily. Similarly his gestures for the prayers were ritualized and remote, eerily like those of Romanesque sculpture, while those for the homily were like the gestures of any Frenchman expounding to a captive audience.

Looking back on that early evening at Chartres, across the space of a few years and a later visit to the cathedral, I think about pilgrimage as a return. More precisely, it seems a ceremonial return to a place to do it honor and to maintain memory. This is, finally, a way of securing the place and its story as a motive for the journey. The word *return* matters here, though it may be misleading at first. The return that is enacted through pilgrimage need not be—perhaps rarely is—within one's own experience or life; it is more powerfully a return within commonly shared practices and memories. Pilgrimage is an act of following. The stone patch set into the tower step is a literal sign of that act. From it I can imagine those who have come before me or will come after. Realizing that in time there will be another patch in that same step, my sense of the present begins to disappear. A pilgrimage site endures in the life of a person paradoxically as a place of transience. You journey there, you are there, and then you leave. If you stay, it is no longer a pilgrimage site; it becomes something close to home. But from that sense of a pilgrim's place comes some understanding that is not transient and fixes it in memory so it can be found again.

What do I make of myself by going to Chartres and climbing the tower repeatedly? Especially since this is the only high place in the world where I have ever known vertigo. Once along the roofline above the northern edge of the nave, and once in the north bell tower, I have had attacks so acute that I could move only by putting my face (eyes closed) to the stone wall and stretching my arms out along it. Why do I go back up these stairs knowing that I might have another attack? It does not always happen, though I can usually summon up just a hint of it. I sometimes think this experience of vertigo is my way toward the sublime or the awesome; it is the place registering itself physically on my body. Perhaps it is my gesture toward Mariolatry, toward the Virgin's allure as intercessor, as mother, as protection against a remorseless god. It is as far as I can go toward Christianity.

This vertigo may be like the experience of pilgrims when they look at the world by distancing themselves from the daily rituals of life. The view from atop Chartres Cathedral is not inspiring; the roofs of houses in the town and the spread of fields beyond seem almost cozily domestic in the neat French landscape. The vertigo comes instead from recognizing that in our time a pilgrimage site exists only as it is made and remade through the desire of each visitor. The place continues to exist, of course, as physical structure, and it retains its associations of meaning. Chartres is stone hewed square and carved, the miraculous blue of its glass, the presence of Mary. But such are now associations as much as dogma, stories as much as doctrine. Chartres holds the imagination as a place of wonder, or more honestly, it holds the imagination of some that visit and return. The cathedral at Chartres is beautifully preserved because it has been a pilgrimage site for so many centuries. Over the twenty years I have visited it, it has never been without scaffolding, and that will always be true. In the fall of 1999 I saw it for the first time without scaffolds on the west facade or the towers, and that will be as unobscured as they will ever be. In another, and more troubling, sense, though, the cathedral will always be a ruin for me because I do not visit it as a place of worship.

In the past no pilgrim to Jerusalem or Santiago de Compostela had ever to answer the question "Why go there?" To announce your destination was to explain your motive. In the twelfth century, this would have been true for Chartres; today it is much less so. A cynic might say that a pilgrimage site is somewhere you bring your faith and leave your money, but that makes it sound too much like a tourist trap. About the places described in this chapter one is very likely to hear "Why go there?" What answers are there to that question? That I am a lost soul in search of my heart's place, or less melodramatically, that I sense in this corner of the earth I might discover something. And so I go there. The vagueness of such answers makes me wish I could say that I was going to Lourdes. For good manners make people keep silent when they suspect illness may be your motive.

A hard dislocation comes from Chartres. For pilgrimage sites now exist less to honor an established religion than to evoke a sense of wonder from visitors. Yet with that recognition comes the admission that a place that moves one visitor to wonder will barely relieve the boredom of another. We are not all bound on the same route to the vertiginous place in our lives. That is why the experience of pilgrimage now seems a private act rather than a communal ceremony, the identification of one soul with a place rather than the anchoring of shared belief in place. The word *pilgrimage* seems archaic and yet necessary in its formality, for we can find our sites and make our pilgrimages only by moving across the landscape alone, keeping our eyes open and our memories filled with the stories we have gathered and the images we have seen.

MEDICINE WHEEL

The site marked on road maps as Medicine Wheel Historic Area rests some 9956 feet atop Medicine Mountain in the Big Horn Range of north-central Wyoming. The town of Cody, which Buffalo Bill built to lure tourists in the 1880s, is some 70 miles southwest along Alternate State Highway 14, the "alternate" meaning that it is partly closed in winter and doesn't serve as a main road. Perhaps fifty miles north of Medicine Wheel as a bird would fly is Little Big Horn in Montana where Custer and his troops met their end, a reminder that no native site in this part of the United States can be read innocently. And about twenty miles due south is the hamlet of Shell, from where Gretel Ehrlich looks at this range: "the benchland tilts up in a series of eroded red-earthed mesas, planed flat on top by a million years of water; behind them, a bold line of muscular scarps rears up ten thousand feet to become the Big Horn Mountains." The scene explains Ehrlich's title for her writer's tour of Wyoming: *The Solace of Open Spaces*.

Perhaps the best way to get to Medicine Wheel is not to triangulate it with these reference points. Instead, find some RVs making their way to Jackson Hole or Yellowstone, and then take the opposite direction. For Medicine Wheel is not in the verdant, fashionable part of the state, and that matters to its story and to why people go there. We went there, the four of us—old traveling companions, writers of various sorts—because the place held out the promise of a long view over the red clay and sage green landscape of northern Wyoming, a scene saved from lunar desolation only by its colors and a thin trace of distant highway.

From the parking area about a mile and a quarter away, you approach Medicine Wheel along a dirt road that leads down a gradual descent of several hundred feet until, at the mid-point, you begin to ascend that same elevation toward a mountain table. In late June, as we followed this road under a lowering sky, there were dense patches of snow packed in shady spots along the way. For much of the year this site and its circle must be buried deep beneath drifts or obscured by wind-driven sheets of snow. It is a hard place, a monument to the sheer force of unmediated nature as it is encountered this far above the floor of the earth.

Other approaches to sacred places offer this same medita-tive pace: the walk, for instance, from the train station up a hill-street until you turn sharply and greet with wonder the west facade of Chartres Cathedral, or the ascent up the Acropolis to the Parthenon, now fenced off for its own pro-tection. But if the approach at Medicine Wheel seems simi-lar, the arrival is utterly different because it does not open to one of the icons of the world, to cathedral or temple. This stone circle in the Big Horn Mountains is not imposing or even especially memorable as a structure. To forestall the obvious, it is far from being Stonehenge in Wyoming. There, what humans have built becomes monumental by rising above the easy grade of Salisbury Plain. The calculus of the site imposes megaliths on the flat earth, and forces us to ask why stones were dragged so far. But here, ten thousand feet up in the Big Horn Mountains, no human construction could seem monumental in the landscape. Medicine Wheel was built low to the ground and does not obstruct the view.

This low circle is, after all, no more than a few stones piled one on top of another. Each is several feet long and of a weight that one or two adults could move easily. At the hub of the wheel is a tall cairn, made of the same stones, from which radiate twenty-eight spokes to a distance of per-haps one hundred feet. Today it is difficult to calculate the dimensions and design of the circle because it is ringed with a barbed-wire fence built against vandalism or, if you feel Medicine Wheel a sacred site, against desecration. Rather than isolating the circle as an artifact from the past, the fence has become part of Medicine Wheel. Visitors tie offerings to it: small cloth bags filled with herbs or tobacco; strips of cloth, some torn impulsively from bandanas or handkerchiefs, some brought purposely to the site; alpine flowers picked nearby and bound together with a thread of wool from a sweater. The fence, meant to protect the site from change, now becomes an altar so visitors may signal their pilgrimage with a ritual gift.

The beauty of the site lies in curve and flow. The metal posts of the fence bend outward to make the wire harder to scale, and there is pleasure in seeing how they obey the circularity of the monument. For those who believe it to have been a sacred observatory to calculate the movements of moon and stars, this design commemorates a cycle that joins earth and sky. These stones might well have been an observatory, a place for calculating the turn of the seasons, and thus for improving the odds of survival, but no stories survive to explain that function.

The site itself helps one to understand the wheel. It is a spacious table-ledge atop the mountain with a few small clumps of fir trees to slow the sweep of the wind as it comes from the north. There is a great sense of openness. Horizon lines all around seem immeasurably distant; other peaks along the ridgeline do not obstruct the view. The valley thousands of feet below is etched starkly visible. Here, the human eye meets a scene that challenges all of its powers of sight. One feels exhilarated but never precarious. The dimensions of the place are generous and extend safely beyond the diameter of the circle.

If Medicine Wheel seems an innocent, poetic name for this construction, consider that it takes its metaphor from a simple machine—the wheel—that was not used by those who built this site. So too "medicine" with its clinical connotations is at best an awkward rendering into English of native beliefs about power and healing. The name "Medicine Wheel" finally says more about the visitors who use it than about the place itself. Yet it matters because it is how we start to interpret this and other monuments that appear across the western United States and Canada. We may not know why these stones were set into this design atop a mountain ridge but we take comfort from them because they suggest a reverence for the site. John Brinckerhoff Jackson, the great portraitist of the American landscape, has called circles and spirals and all such constructions "signs of our sense of responsibility for the survival of the earth and its people."

Like most travelers, I have spent a great deal of time in other people's holy places. The list of churches, temples, synagogues, mosques, shrines, altars, cairns, mounds, dancing grounds, pyramids, glades, springs, and the like that I have sought out for their stories of place would run for pages and could perhaps give some sense of why the sacred can draw us even—perhaps especially—when we do not share the faith of that site. These are often the official sights of a place, too, because they were built to command a scene, to fill a landscape, to force themselves on visitors in order to win their souls. As one without religious belief, I find these holy places at times terrifying, but I do not enjoy seeing them desecrated. A young man smoking inside Chartres Cathedral is one of my painful memories of travel because his gesture, and it was meant to be taken as a gesture by the way he stylized the lighting and smoking of his cigarette, showed a willed refusal to be moved by the place. It was an act of vandalism, no less angry for being ephemeral.

At Medicine Wheel the site is wonderfully clean; visitors put their refuse, what little there was of it that late afternoon, in containers. All they leave behind are strips of cloth tied to the barbed-wire fence and outside it small piles of sunflower seeds set within elaborate designs made from pebbles. As the difference of scale resolves itself, these designs emerge as tiny versions of the large circle, imitations made to enact what some visitor imagines to have been the ritual of the place. There is a reverence about these small circles and their piles of seeds that made me think of lighting candles in a cathedral. Yet there is also a difference that speaks to the Americanness of Medicine Wheel, for each circle of seeds and pebbles is built to some private, unarticulated spiritual end, while each candle lit at Chartres is a ritual to implore the mercy of the Virgin.

Medicine Wheel has become a holy site for contemporary travelers because it has no established meaning. Without doctrine or dogma, without being a sanctuary for a minor divinity or local saint, it draws pilgrims in search of a site where they can root their own beliefs in earth they believe sacred because it is unfouled by formulas of accepted belief. Those who visited Medicine Wheel when we were there did not look at all like tourists on the streets of such Wyoming towns as Cody and Sheridan. For this part of America, they were remarkably free of cowboy myth and adornment. Rather than Stetsons and silver belt-buckles, these visitors blended old hippie ponchos and organic jewelry with hi-tech sneakers and Gore-Tex protective gear. After driving miles on the interstate, they seemed to have found at Medicine Wheel a pilgrimage site in ways that those who walked through the Wyoming tourist towns in Old West regalia had not. The visitors at Medicine Wheel looked as if they were rapturous or, perhaps truer, as if they wanted above all else to be rapturous. What drew all of these visitors to the place puzzled me until my wife Georgina suggested that Medicine Wheel had become a stop on the New Age map of America where those with mystical aspirations could absorb the aura of the setting and locate themselves without feeling the hand of dogma at their throats; Emerson, who taught us to turn the sublime into our American faith, would have understood the impulse of the place.

That these visitors were pilgrims in the strict sense of the term was confirmed for me when I returned home and found in a local New Age bookstore *Sacred Sites: A Traveler's Guide to North America's Most Powerful, Mystic Landmarks*. There, with a blotchy photograph that made Medicine Wheel look like a weed-filled backyard, were several pages of pseudoscientific blather about celestial observatories, prophetic star-formations, bands of extraterrestrial little people, and so forth: "The medicine wheels may have been built only to declare the time of the sacred Sun Dance. Or, they may be about something not yet imagined. Surely the sky-gazers were watching for more than the sun. Something out there was very holy indeed." In the midst of this breathless prose appears the significant claim: "Surely only the most spiritually and scientifically gifted of the tribe gathered at the medicine wheels." This is the "surely" of the true believer, ready to dismiss others as unworthy. Nor is it a claim about the past and those who built that stone circle. Rather it is about the present and those who visit Medicine Wheel in search of spiritual vision. The irony of this claim, as it grows into absurdity, is simply that no one knows what was believed or practiced or observed on that mountaintop. And, as anyone can see who visits it, there is room there for many hundreds, even thousands of pilgrims. Nothing about the place excludes or limits; it is open and inviting, at least on a June day.

As you leave the place, and walk that same dirt road back to your car, you must finally confront the sight you have avoided throughout your visit: a radar dome on the next summit along the ridgeline. According to a tourist guidebook with no avowed interest in spirituality, it serves the Federal Aviation Authority by tracking the weather and flight paths in this part of the country. The same book calls it a "sacrilege," a desecration of a holy site. It is easy to agree with its piety; the dome is ugly, discordant, flanked by shabby outbuildings that litter the scene. Here, where there is so much space, so many high elevations, why did that dome have to be built a mile or so from Medicine Wheel?

Then, with a doubling vision, a pattern emerges, a harmony between the ring of stone and that dome set to read weather patterns along the horizon line. Both command a long vista across landscape and sky, both turn with a circular pattern to see all around them. They are machines for calculating the uncontrollable, for finding some knowledge to survive amid the harshness of the natural world. The New Age pilgrims do not climb the hill and adorn the radar dome with cloth or tobacco; it has no medicine or magic for them. They reject its claims to knowledge because it violates the landscape. Yet nothing could offer greater proof that we need, as much as we love, the distant knowledge that comes of the long view across a landscape.

Medicine Wheel reminded me of what I already knew as a medievalist: one of the most tenacious stories that can cling to a place is the promise of spiritual enlightenment. If we go to where Thomas à Beckett was murdered in Canterbury Cathedral we know we can gain solace from it as a holy site because we have read *The Canterbury Tales*. We go there, as did Chaucer's pilgrims, because a familiar narrative carries with it a fixed and shared sense of place. Yet Medicine Wheel as a site within the spiritual landscape of the contemporary United States suggests that a pilgrimage site can exist without a fixed story and that it may indeed be all the more revered for lacking such a story.

Medicine Wheel endures today not to commemorate a holy faith, for it has no identifiable communal meaning, but to create new stories that will sustain those who tell and hear them. Or, as Charles Doughty said of the Arabian Desert: "Monuments of human hands . . . are a comfortable sight in this Titanic landscape." That a constructed site can provide the consolations of story in a titanic landscape beyond human scale is a deeply appealing notion. What travelers to a site like Medicine Wheel can finally find there, once it is freed of pseudospiritualist cant, may be the possibility that stories of a place can reveal the same qualities as does the place itself. Medicine Wheel evokes light-filled contrasts and wind-swept clarity, stories that elude finality to tell of the long and open view.

Fast-Food America

When writers claim to avoid interstates and fast-food restaurants in order to find the real America, get set for foolishness about old-time dialects, country crafts, and characters of the sort they don't make anymore. Or so the writer will assure you, and praise himself (almost always it is a man) for being ballsy enough to turn off the four-lane and find real folks rooted in their region who cannot be confused with people three states away or even on the other side of the mountain. These are people, he will promise, that it is worth traveling to see because their identities remain rooted in the place and its past.

Most of these books are unbearably certain that you must follow the backroads or else be damned to a postmodern hell where everything looks the same and nothing has the savor of its place. And where, of course, there are no stories. It is not that these travel writers take backroads to find the vivid, the salty, the forgotten that is so annoying; it is that they deny other roads lead there. If you read enough of these books, you'll realize that Americans like to locate their exotic in a lost pastoral world. Although less ponderous than most, William Least Heat Moon's *Blue Highways* is the best-known recent example of the genre:

> On the old highway maps of America, the main routes were red and the back roads blue. Now even the colors are changing. But in those brevities just before dawn and a little after dusk—times neither day nor night—the old roads return to the sky some of its color. Then, in truth, they carry a mysterious cast of blue, and it's that time when the pull of the blue highway is strongest, when the open road is a beckoning, a strangeness, a place where a man can lose himself.

Instead of a raft on the Mississippi or a whaling ship in the South Seas, Least Heat Moon made do with a Ford van he named "Ghost Dancer." He could roam nineteenth-century America because he avoided those interstates that burn their way across the map with only passing regard to topography or culture; he found his curious, gnarled characters by losing himself on blue highways. But you must remember, when reading his book, that he taught literature before setting out and knew this country's need to locate the authentic in little hamlets and sleepy burgs: Edwin Arlington Robinson in Maine, Sherwood Anderson in Ohio, Faulkner in

125

Mississippi, Cather in Nebraska, Capote in Kansas. But each of them knew, as few travel writers of the backroads sort ever do, that small-town life is no more authentic than life elsewhere. They put their places on the map precisely because they avoided nostalgia.

I think about this sometimes while drinking coffee in a fast-food place along an interstate. Usually, I've driven too far that day and need to slow down; the discipline of hot coffee is that it takes more time than a cold drink. Chain places are preferable because they clean the toilets and keep the place anonymous. They remind me that the most enviable of travelers—adaptable and graceful medievals like Ibn Battuta or Marco Polo—stuck to the main roads, the caravan routes, the pilgrimage ways. On the beaten track, they found what they needed: the exchange of goods, the ebb and flow of human beings moving about for all imaginable reasons, confirmation that life lies in motion and transfer. They knew that routes, like places, have their stories.

And so, on an early winter afternoon in a McDonalds off I-90 in Erie, Pennsylvania, I looked up from my coffee to see a Japanese family settle into the next booth. They negotiated the business of fast-food America with perfect style despite limited fluency in English. It seemed little different for them here than in a McDonalds at home. The beauty of chain places is that they keep us from making fools of ourselves when we travel. As the parents spoke to each other in Japanese, one said "Cleveland" and pointed to a map; then the other said "Toledo" and pointed a few inches to the left. "Cleveland" and "Toledo" passed back and forth as they looked at their watches and then at their two kids. They decided to stop for the night in Cleveland, or at least they turned to it in their guidebook.

This act of locating oneself on the road, of planning the next stop, occurs millions of times each day around the world. Trivial as this example seems, it made me wonder how others in that McDonalds located themselves on the edge of the interstate. There were teenagers in sweatshirts emblazoned "Penn State," "Yale," "Georgia Tech," "Indiana"; a girl in a cheerleader jacket that read "Knoch"; a man in his forties, my age, in a shirt with "Dave" over one pocket and "Master Mold Co." over the other. Some came in with the names of sports teams or sneaker companies across their fronts and were served at the counter by blond teenagers with name-tags that said Amy, Katrina, and Melissa, and by a Latino named Joe. Yes, it could have been anywhere in America. The colleges and teams would have different names elsewhere but the need to declare an allegiance would remain. One could say, cynically, that they emblazon themselves with the identities of others because they are displaced and yet still need to belong somewhere. So they choose whatever lies closest to home. In Erie, it's "Pirates," "Steelers," "Pitt," "Penn State," "Slippery Rock."

At such moments, it is easy to feel superior to people on the edge of the interstate and to cherish instead the lure of the old days and backroads. But that will not help anyone understand place in America today. Do we rely on these emblazonings because of the loneliness of these spaces, the certainty that we will meet only strangers along the way, the need to state where we come from literally or spiritually? Is it that the interstate becomes a metaphor for our condition of being in transit between places and finally at home in none of them? Or are the emblazonings tokens of the journey, like the badges made of base metal that medieval pilgrims back from Santiago de Compostela or Rome or Jerusalem wore on their breasts? These badges testified to the distances pilgrims would go to honor their faith or atone for their sins. They proclaimed that the wearer's business on the highway was holy and thus to be respected. I do not know that the people driving I-90 were searching for some holy shrine of their imagining or that they hoped to find a place with its own savor somewhere along the anonymous road. I could only feel that travelers and writers who turned off the highway for the old roads were distancing themselves from any possibility of speaking about how we travel now.

Fast-food America has its stories. The place itself can seem a never-changing belt along the interstate of neon, grease, sugar, diesel fumes. Most of it is ugly, little is built to last out the decade, and all of it obeys the imperative of speed that is, in America, the creation of space. The traveler's law of thermodynamics, should it ever be written, would relate the desire for speed to the distance that must be traversed. That law would also predict casualties along the way. In a Kentucky Fried Chicken off I-44 in Sullivan, Missouri, I found a graffito on the back of a stall door that could only be read as you sat on the toilet: "Because it's fried shit, that's why." It was, in the idiom of the road, a cautionary message about too much driving and too much fast food. And if you wondered what it meant, you hadn't spent enough time in transient America.

Sentimental travelers speak of old diners as shrines on the highway; they had eccentricities of style, a suspicion of strangers, the best pie for miles. To see this nostalgia for the diner celebrated in, remarkably, a Burger King is worth a long drive in itself. So go to Sheridan, Wyoming, off I-90 in the eastern and less fashionable part of the state. The place looks like every other Burger King: plastic, easy to clean, comfortable enough for a brief stop. The locals find it a useful breakfast club. The menu you already know from your hometown. But along one wall hangs a group of pictures meant to remake the place in an older image. "The Runaway" by Norman Rockwell shows a benevolent cop and a little boy sitting next to each other on stools in a diner. Under the boy's is his bindlestaff, his hobo gear. The story is simple: cop, boy, diner all belong to a time when boys did boys' mischief in running away, cops remembered their own boyhoods when bringing them home, and the counterman was a friend to both. Next is a stark black-and-white photograph of a diner countertop by Paul Hoffman that makes the usual salt-and-pepper shakers, chrome napkin dispensers, ashtrays, and the like seem chicly monumental. Finally, a poster from the O.K. Harris Gallery in New York's SoHo, of all places, shows a painting by Ralph Going of a diner in a landscape much like that outside this same Burger King.

The message was clear: the diners you miss from your childhood, or (more likely) from memories of someone else's, have been reconstructed here in the franchise restaurant. The rituals of life continue in the landscape, as you will discover if you listen to the conversations around you: the exchange of news between a soldier's wife home for a visit and her former high-school teacher; the time-worn stories passed among retired ranchers idling away the June morning when they would rather have been out working; the flow of greetings and news that sustains life and makes for community. If you sit there long enough with your coffee and are not intrusive—it helps to read the local paper; you will seem less alien above a familiar headline—then you will see that all of this coming and going is the life of the place. Here in a building that looks like thousands of others, the transient is anchored to some sense of home, the global is made local, the stories of the place get told beneath pictures of old diners, the travel writer finds material. It's as close to the real America as anyone will ever get, or could survive finding.

The Middle Prairies

Writing of a dry, reserved landscape like Nebraska's Sand Hills requires a love for the quiet and restrained. This landscape is, to echo a phrase by Max Frisch, a place with no Baedeker stars. It is too understated to attract the traveler in search of the esoteric. Driving on Nebraska Highway 2 through a belt of low sand hills, you spend hours looking at terrain that in the early nineteenth century gave rise to the myth that America had, like Australia and Asia, a Great Desert at its heart. This stretch of road runs roughly east-west for perhaps 250 miles and can be done in an afternoon, though it is good to get out and walk off the pavement to feel how resistant and slow the going would be by animal or foot. In his *Oregon Trail*, Francis Parkman in ways that still hold described "the Platte and the Desert" as he saw the scene in 1846:

> At length we gained the summit, and the long-expected valley of the Platte lay before us. . . . It was right welcome; strange too, and striking to the imagination, and yet it had not one picturesque or beautiful feature; nor had it any of the features of grandeur, other than its vast extent, its solitude and its wildness.

For the traveler bent on passing through Nebraska quickly, this landscape will seem almost punishingly tedious. Even the name disappoints, for these hills are no more than a series of gentle rises and easy slopes that would seem table-flat a hundred miles farther west into Wyoming.

Yet if you simply look and forget where you are not, the landscape will draw you in until you wonder if there *are* boring or featureless landscapes. The towns on Highway 2 as you head west have names that map the region's history: Ravenna, Hazard, Broken Bow, Anselmo, Seneca, Whitman, Hyannis, Ellsworth, Antioch, Alliance. The road runs loosely parallel to the North Platte River, though at least twenty, and sometimes as much as fifty, miles can separate the two. Along that path of road and river run great stories. The Oregon Trail as well as the Mormon Trail to Deseret followed the North Platte; at Scottsbluff near the western edge of the state the easy gradient of the prairies begins to give way to jagged desert. There, the hard traveling began. Today the railroad lines and interstate pass along the North Platte, still obeying the chosen way west.

Willa Cather's lyrical novels of frontier settlement, My Antonia and O Pioneers!, are set in the fertile land along the river and south toward Kansas. A few hours from the Sand Hills in that direction is Red Cloud, where Cather spent her youth and fled as soon as she could. Today, as if to repay her for that betrayal, Red Cloud adorns its old houses with signs identifying them as settings for her novels. The literary tourists come, as we did, look around, eat a richly marbled steak at the Palace Restaurant, photograph themselves beneath the store-sign for "Sacks Fourth Avenue." But that day, driving through the Sand Hills with only a few scattered animals grazing and the rare long-legged bird lifting off from a dune-marsh, I kept thinking of the mad Ivar who, in O Pioneers!, cannot easily abide human company and seeks refuge in the Sand Hills because they were fit only for the mystical, the mad, and the lost.

This scene, now so forgotten but once at the center of America's mythic geography, makes me wonder if there is anything such as a featureless landscape. It is good to remember that nineteenth-century travelers heading west would make wide detours to avoid this so-called desert because it was believed to stretch for hundreds of miles north and south beyond its actual range. This memory makes me hesitate to call a landscape featureless because, to those with local knowledge, it will be defining, elusively complex, sustaining.

In a landscape like the Sand Hills, a small defile or a creekbed with cottonwoods growing along its edge can seem as alluring as a starred attraction in any guidebook. Its contours, its rise and fall, its scales of difference are themselves engaging. The key to being in the American landscape, where so much is monumental, is to calculate comforting scales for measuring a scene. There are in the Sand Hills intimacies of gradation, curving flanks along hillsides that rise a few feet above the groundline, subtle shadings of golden browns, burnt tans, and sage grays. In the fall, the Sand Hills have a pied beauty, a brindling of grasses, low scrub, and dying flowers broken by shallow marshpools that reflect the sky. All is in motion—clouds, water, grass—because nothing rises high enough to break the wind. The terrain seems blasted by the constant motion of weather. Strands of barbed wire along the roadside mark this as grazing land, as do the signs pointing up dirt roads to ranches and cattle companies. This is desolate country where drivers keep their gastanks topped off.

The state road is the fastest way through this country; it is, in fact, the only way marked east-west on the map. Here, roads are where they are because they follow the path of least resistance. The highways flank old wagon trails or railbeds, which cover the original paths in turn. If you look closely, you can spot remnants of the old ways but they are being reclaimed by the grass and scrub that are the enduring features of the place. Each of these courses avoids the most difficult terrain, which for us, in our traveler's vanity and motor vehicles, is the landscape with notable features. Tracing one of these old routes west along a modern highway is to honor the ways topography imposes its logic on an enormous landscape; the old choices continue to set the route for those who follow.

There is a characteristic rhythm to traveling in the American West: quiet lengths of steady driving as you push 75 or 80 miles per hour are broken by moments of curiosity and engagement in small towns. You get gas, take a piss, buy a soda, look for something that will be the story of the place as you see it strung a house or two deep along the state road. For all that you look around and strike up a conversation with the cashier at the gas station in the hope of getting a colorful phrase or detail for the account you plan to write, the rhythm forces you back on the road. For that is the logic of the landscape: that every fact of life here hangs on the distance you must travel to get somewhere else.

Crossing the Sand Hills, I felt a sense of familiarity that came less from the shape of the terrain than from its brindled colors. At first the likeness seemed to Oklahoma but it was too sandy for that. The answer came when a roadsign gave the distance to Hyannis and then I knew this region was what Cape Cod looked like before it became a resort. Or, perhaps more truthfully, that for a moment some settlers who looked along the run of low sand hills saw it was like the Cape because, heartsick, they needed to see it that way. A guide to Nebraska placenames could confirm my guess that this Hyannis commemorates a small town on the upper arm of the Cape, but traveler's instinct tells me it does. So I compromise, and learn that, among the tens of thousands of places indexed in the *Times Atlas of the World*, only two are named Hyannis: in Massachusetts and Nebraska.

And then comes a dim memory from Henry Beston's *The Outermost House* (1928), a book that endures because it allows us to remember Cape Cod as a place of elemental solitude, that there was one grove of cottonwood trees on the Cape. The seeds were brought back from Kansas when a few residents who had left the Cape for a better life on the prairies returned because, Beston says, they were "homesick for the sea." Perhaps others who went to Nebraska found solace for their homesickness in the Sand Hills. Pumping gas in Hyannis, I could not articulate these connections but they were the start of the story of this place.

The way names fall across the land affects the way we travel. On that same trip in Nebraska, where a stretch of Highway 2 west of Ravenna was being rebuilt and all traffic rerouted through that small town with its name (if only that) redolent of the Adriatic, a sign greeted us: "WELCOME DETOURISTS STOP AND SHOP RAVENNA." The sign was locally made with awkward stenciling on a 4' x 8' sheet of plywood; the sentiment was so purely chamber of commerce that we wondered if there really were anything wrong with the highway or if we were being lured into the business district to spend money. But then the sign came to seem a gift as we headed into a landscape as reserved and unspectacular as the Sand Hills. We were that day, the four of us, heading west and far from any famous sight, detourists who stopped beside this sign to photograph ourselves couple by couple. Now, on our desks, these photographs remind us of trips taken by pilgrims to quiet places where, at the edge of nowhere famous, they hoped to draw the romantic and strange from the familiar and modest.

ORKNEY, THE RING OF BRODGAR

The photo on the postcard shows a ring of stone slabs, some 125 "megalithic yards" (103.6 meters) in diameter, that rests between the arms of two encroaching lochs. The light in the picture suggests a late afternoon of changeable weather; the clouds, heavy and metallic like pewter, are underlit with a band of silver as the sun begins to drop in the long June day. The thirty-six surviving stones of the ring's original sixty are set plumb to the ground and many still reach their original height of fifteen feet. Their dense grayness makes them seem massive. On edge, though, they are breathtakingly thin, some no more than five or six inches. It is remarkable to grasp one of these stones edgewise, to sense for a moment how it might have been held as it was set into place millenia ago. The Ring of Brodgar becomes more imposing when viewed broadside, though it never seems to have emerged, as does Stonehenge, from the earth below. With their rakishly angled tops, the stones at Brodgar have a grace that suggests air as much as earth.

In this postcard, the land, sky, and water of Brodgar arrange themselves across a palette of grays until the stones shade into black. The photo, it appears, was taken from a low angle that makes the stones rear up like the prow of a raked Viking ship. This image is anachronistic, for the stones predate the Viking presence on Orkney by several thousand years, but it captures an elegance of form common to both. The postcard illustrates all that we mean when we speak of the brooding mystery of place.

In truth, this postcard comes from memory and a few of my own photographs. I wish it existed because then there might be some text on the reverse, even a few words hastily scrawled, to narrate the scene or evoke its story. The physical presence of the Ring is inescapable on the landscape, as is the attempt to calculate the human labor that was given to its construction. By the reckoning of archaeologists, it took some 80,000 hours simply to dig the surrounding ditch in the bedrock. Because we know so little about it, the Ring of Brodgar has, like Medicine Wheel in the Wyoming mountains, attracted all sorts of claims: it was a meeting ground for the tribe, a dance theater to honor the ancient goddess, an observatory to measure celestial movements, a field of memory for travel writers, a landing zone for extraterrestrials.

The Ring's mystery should be all the more solvable because it is not alone on Orkney. Within an easy walk on the island are other constructions, other clues to the long prehistory of the place: the Stones of Stenness, a smaller and now fragmented ring set in a sheep pasture that you enter by a stile; and the great domed mound of Maes Howe that once served as a burial chamber and is now open to visitors (no photography allowed inside). Vikings returning from Jerusalem in the twelfth century bivouacked in Maes Howe and left behind graffiti sketches of a lion, an otter, and a serpent, as well as praise for the beautiful Ingigerth. But the presence of these other stone survivals—ruins is too dismissive a word for their beauty—only complicates our questions about the Ring of Brodgar. For it is not alone on the landscape and thus cannot be explained by some exception.

The notes I scribbled on a late June afternoon beneath a restless sky are awkward attempts to set the Ring of Brodgar into its landscape:

> Orkney sites one after the stratified other: neolithic Skara Braes, Maes Howe and stone rings, last the buildings of Viking Orkney. all built with skill, patience, a sense of wonder to last out the years.

A sense of craft all the more moving for the austere, desolate
setting. not a place of abundance where craft comes easy.

What did Vikings make of these monuments? they left traces
inside Maes Howe, did they wonder about the rings? were
they *enta geweorc*, the "work of giants," as Old English
poets would say?

Travel as seeing the work of giants; history as knowing that
giants left traces.

Do later writers say anything about them? *Orkneyinga Saga*?
Edwin Muir, born near here?

My notes were hasty attempts to hold on to the place, to
sense where its story might be. There are places so old in
mystery that their endurance across time is more compelling and more reassuring than any answer about their origin
could ever be. That is what makes us choose to visit such
a place.

Returning home, I reread the early thirteenth-century
Orkneyinga Saga and found nothing about stone circles or
burial chambers. The saga tells about the murderous dynas-
tic feuds among the earls of Orkney and about the treacherous currents among the islands of the archipelago. But traces
left by earlier inhabitants seem not to belong to its story.
In his *Autobiography* (1954), the Orcadian poet Edwin
Muir remembered playing as a boy on the ruins of a Viking
fort near the family farmstead but said nothing about
the Ring of Brodgar or Maes Howe. The small island of
Wyre was for him "a universal landscape over which Abra-
ham and Achilles and Ulysses and Tristram and all sorts of
pilgrims passed; and Troy was associated with the Castle, a
mere green mound, near my father's house." That Muir's

memories were shaped by the landscape of European epic rather than stories about the Orcadian past seems a cautionary lesson about the places we select for our pilgrimages, for journeys we make from our private rather than communal being.

Of the writers I found, only the contemporary American poet, Emily Hiestand, troubled to reflect on her encounter with the Ring of Brodgar:

> Whatever their original shape, the stones have weathered into asymmetrical, lean, dark, and skeletal forms that resemble the sculptures of Alberto Giacometti. These are natives whose character is the meeting of time, rock, wind, rain, and sun; the contours and surfaces and hubris wept away in undulating ripples until each stone is an unmistakable individual, dignified and acquainted with sorrow; there is a ghost, a fat one, an avuncular soul, a stooped figure bearing a baby on its back.

Even if the stones are ghosts, Hiestand seems to say, they have their stories and may tell them to us if we see how they have metamorphosed over time. Her desire to read these stones is infinitely moving. But these stones cannot become attendant spirits of place, austerely minimalist figures on the verge of speech. For it is not these stories that trouble me, but rather those that were being told as the stones were raised by people we know little about. The stories told as the site was being made are lost.

That these stories about Brodgar can never be known should protect it from travelers in search of one last unwritten place. As an adjective, *unwritten* may be more polite than "unspoiled" but it has the same vanity about it, that drive to profit by glibly narrating the wondrous sites of the earth. There are certain places where words should fail us, where we cannot shape a story. This silence lies not in our inability to find words for the sublimity of a place, that oldest of poetic excuses. It lies in a stony reticence that certain sites, like the Ring of Brodgar, impose on us. We owe them more than a journal entry scribbled with breathless musings about our pilgrimage.

CHAPTER 5

The Place of History: Berlin

The traveler's temptation is to fix a place with a phrase and then be done with it. Sometimes, the phrase works: Florence lives in its stones, as Mary McCarthy saw; Paris remains the capital of the nineteenth century, as Walter Benjamin knew. Offering such a phrase for Berlin seems riskier because what happened there has happened much more recently. It is a place where history is not yet history or, more exactly, where the past has a way of returning just when it seemed possible to file it away as dead and gone.

When Berliners asked me in 1997, usually with some apprehension, how I liked their city, they would immediately understand my response that "like" was not the word for the place. But that easy point made, one still needed to talk about the city. At such moments I fell into a phrase that seemed to satisfy Berliners and that evaded the force of their question: Berlin was history interrupted by construction. And if I said this in Mitte, the central district of the city, there was a quick nod of recognition, for everywhere there was construction and reconstruction, the vibration of heavy equipment, the Arabic, Polish, and English spoken by workers on scaffolds. Walking through Mitte, your shoes pick up a thin coat of dust from its building sites. Here, construction-watching has been made into an art form. From the elevated "Red Box" overlooking Potsdamer Platz, where once there was only the "death strip," you can gaze out at what is called, in the inevitable formula, whether English or German, "the largest construction site in the world." Here the cranes have been, quite literally, choreographed to perform a ballet of mechanical movement as a public performance.

For all that Berlin is a spectacle to enjoy, you realize after a time that the money and energy thrown into constructing and reconstructing the city are no more than an interruption. After the equipment and workers are gone, the corporate headquarters are finished and the art deco buildings refurbished, memories of all that happened here will remain. The Wall is gone, but its path will be marked for years to come by a run of new construction from Checkpoint Charlie to Potsdamer Platz to the River Spree. The enormous buildings of the late 1990s will divide the reunified Berlin of the future as surely as the city was divided from 1961 to 1989 by the Wall. For all their postmodern glamour, the corporate palaces of Daimler-Benz, SONY, and others will mark the map of Berlin like scar tissue. The wound may close, but its trace will remain. In the meantime, it is necessary to buy, through building and rebuilding, some time away from all the questions that haunt one about the city.

During June 1997 I taught courses in medieval studies to graduate students at the Humboldt University in what had been the eastern sector of the city. That they were all in their mid-twenties or older matters because they were on the verge of adulthood when the *Wende* occurred in 1989. It affected them profoundly because they were raised in East

Germany. In the shifting vernacular of the place, they were born Ossies. This portrait of Berlin comes largely from conversations with these students, conversations that were all the more charged because they occurred at a university in the center of Mitte. To talk about the writing of history in this setting was not a routine academic exercise for any of us. When we left the building on Unter den Linden where class met we could walk west toward the Brandenburg Gate and the Reichstag, or east toward the Palace of the Republic, built by the communist government on the site of what had been the old imperial palace. Near where we got coffee between classes was the square where in 1933 students burned books by Jews and other dangerous authors. Across Unter den Linden was the Neue Wache, the "New Watch," a Prussian guardhouse that has been made into a memorial for all the suffering and death brought into the world by Germany during the twentieth century.

Reading scholars whose lives and works had been twisted by the Germany of the 1930s and 1940s meant moving beyond the ostensible subject of medieval studies. To discuss Erich Auerbach, forced into exile by the Nazis in 1935; or E. R. Curtius, who spent the war as an internal émigré writing a visionary encyclopedia of European medieval literature; or Marc Bloch, who led the Resistance in Lyons and was executed by the Gestapo in 1944—these discussions led to questions about the relations between a scholar's life and the writing of history. And these questions had everything to do with the place where they were asked. As the narrator of Christa Wolf's story "Unter den Linden" says, "I had always suspected that this street leads into unknown depths."

Walking on Friedrichstrasse from Unter den Linden to the train station, a distance of three or four city blocks, means weaving back and forth from one sidewalk to the other to avoid building sites. You make progress but not in a straight-forward way. Each day, it seems, the barriers have been shifted slightly, so today's route is not the same as yester-day's, nor will it be the same as tomorrow's.

These subtle shifts in daily route force shifts in the way you look at the same scene. Crossing at mid-street instead of at a corner means looking at the flow of buildings in ways not possible the day before. Changes in the urban landscape appear: as one building comes down, the view of another opens and what was hidden emerges, though it may soon disappear from view as a new building rises. The history of the city gets played out in its architectural styles. Nine-teenth- and early-twentieth-century buildings that survived the bombing are being restored, and new glass boxes are being erected in the open spaces. From a bench along Unter den Linden you can watch a steady flow of flatbed trucks loaded with plasterboard, dumptrucks filled with torn-up masonry or paving, and cement mixers churning away. The sign on one truck could serve as a motto for this new Berlin: *für Bau und Aufbau* (for construction and reconstruction). When you look up from street level, the horizon line is filled with construction cranes swinging their loads. From one spot on the edge of Potsdamer Platz I counted twenty-nine cranes before the light turned green and I moved on.

There are disconcerting, even shocking, juxtapositions in Mitte between the most elegant Art Deco hotel covered with sexy nymphs in stone and the shabbiest, poured con-crete, pre-fab building left over from the GDR, one of the ubiquitous *Plattenbauten*. It would be hard, if you did not know the narrative of Berlin, to comprehend how it hap-pened that such buildings came to stand next to each other.

For how could any one place have such impossibly different senses of how to build and thus of how to live?

The most troubled site of construction and reconstruction in Mitte is the Palace of the Republic that sits on the far end of Unter den Linden from the Brandenburg Gate. Occupying the site of what had been the imperial palace until it was razed after being bombed in World War II, the Palace of the Republic today stands empty and abandoned because it is poisoned with asbestos. Surrounded by a chain-link fence it seems enormous, evocative, too eloquent a relic from the communist era to be treated merely as a building. And so, overcharged with symbolism, it sits while Berliners argue about whether it should be torn down, because it is ugly and contaminated and thus a reminder of the communist past, or be restored, because it was a place where people enjoyed themselves at restaurants and bowling alleys and thus a reminder of the communist past. Or, and this is no cheap paradox, that it should be preserved for exactly the reasons some would tear it down, or torn down for exactly the reasons some would preserve it.

Today, the bronze mirror-glass facade of the Palace reflects little except the tour buses parked in what was once Marx-Engels Place. They pile in there, their drivers happy to escape the snarl of Berlin traffic. Wisecracks about the locomotive of history being replaced by tourist buses forever parked in front of the abandoned Palace of the Republic are easy, almost too easy, to make. More eloquent was the scene I witnessed one afternoon of a group of ten-year-olds on an excursion with their teachers. As they walked the length of the building, almost two hundred meters along the chain-link fence, not one of them stopped to look up at the Palace. Even ten years earlier that would have been a destination for their school trip; now it's only the edge of a dusty square filled with buses, piles of building material, dumpsters.

The Deutsche Bank on the corner of Unter den Linden and Charlottenstrasse has, by contrast, been impeccably restored to its pre–World War II condition. Its immaculate stonework and polished metal proclaim it to be the headquarters of a long-established concern, though one that has been absent from the neighborhood for some time due to unavoidable circumstances. But it is back now, and the parade of black Mercedes-Benzes is there in front to assure us that important business is being conducted within. To complete the restoration, a wall of plate-glass has been erected across the facade of the bank's upper four stories. The striking effect seals the building off from the city as if it were on display behind a museum case. This glass suggests a desire to ward off the workings of time and history, to exist hermetically apart from the grime and pollution that fill the Berlin air, once famously pure and now redolent with complicated odors. Looking at that wall—no less impermeable for being transparent—reminds you that banks are well practiced in the art of historical accommodation.

Throughout Mitte the air smells of partially burned diesel fuel from the rumble of construction equipment and heavy trucks; its scent mixes strangely well with the occasional whiff of human waste that comes up from the sewers. That odor, Berliners joke, lets even the blind know where they are on the old map of the city: east or west. In Berlin, a scene will arrange itself with such metaphorical, even allegorical brilliance that you wonder if there is any literal being or meaning to the place. Take something as common as this: the east side of the German Historical Museum, once the old Prussian Arsenal, completed in 1730, is covered with scaffolding and plastic sheeting as it undergoes renovation.

In this, it is no different from hundreds of other buildings in Mitte. All of the building's side is veiled, yet from above the sheeting appear statues of historical and mythical figures. It is, on the face of it, no more than stonework being repaired. But the eye cannot avoid reading it as a scene about the workings of history in this part of the world. No covering completely hides the past, some trace escapes, and is all the more revealing for being incomplete. To use the title of Brian Ladd's thoughtful book, one can speak of "the ghosts of Berlin," but they do not haunt with a wraith-like mystery. The danger of looking at Berlin is captured nastily by the joke Berliners tell of the American tourist, the one who wanted to know why Hitler built the Reichstag so close to the Wall. It can be very hard to construct a stable chronology for a city in which buildings and monuments remain unchanged as physical structures but acquire with each change of government new symbolic purposes.

The plan, after the Bolsheviks came to power in Russia, was to make Berlin the capital of the permanent revolution. It never happened. Karl Liebknecht and Rosa Luxemburg were murdered in 1919. Then came the Weimar Republic, Hitler, the GDR—enough to make one think at times that Berlin has been the capital of the twentieth century. Yet even here, on Walter Benjamin's homeground, it will not work to follow his gesture of choosing a city as capital for a century. And Berlin is certainly not the Paris of the last century, the paradise of the *flâneur*. For a foreigner, it is not easy to maintain that ironic detachment. Every site impinges, every attempt to look away from one site brings you face to face with another. If Berlin marks anything in our time, it is as one of the places where the hopes of the twentieth century went to die. And how do you build a monument for that?

When I told my students that Marc Bloch was considered by some American scholars to be a Marxist historian because he related feudal society and its social institutions to the agricultural means of production, they laughed. Having been educated in East Germany, they all knew by rote a Marxist historiography in service of the party line. They understood that Bloch's subtle explorations into the relationship, for example, between the boredom of the knightly classes and the development of chivalric romance shared nothing with the grand schemes of history they had been taught. About this, they were articulate and shrewd. When we talked about the historiography that Bloch rejected in the 1920s—that of kings and wars, of history as one great event after another—they seemed somewhat puzzled. For that sense of history was familiar to them only through the caricatures of capitalist thinking they had learned before the *Wende*.

That reading medieval history might have some direct political value broke through at the very end of the term when a student, her eyes blurred with tears, spoke about what it meant to read Marc Bloch and E. R. Curtius, Georges Duby and Jacques Le Goff. From them, she said, she learned that history was more than a slave uprising led by Spartacus, or peasant revolts during the Middle Ages, or the failed movements of 1848: history could be something more complex, less eschatological, than a rehearsal for the Russian Revolution. What she had been denied as a student, she said simply, was the past. And of the medievalists we read, it was Curtius she cited because he had withdrawn during the Nazi years to write his *European Literature and the Latin Middle Ages*, a massive study that argued that the unitary nature of European civilization derived from a commonly held classical and medieval tradition. It was a tradition, he argued, that had shaped alike all of the Western European nations fighting each other in the 1940s. Curtius's book stands as an implicit polemic against all claims of German exceptionalism. This student's praise for Curtius drew, as well, on her memories of people in the GDR who had kept alive senses of the past other than those that had been officially sanctioned. For, like Curtius, such people would have struggled to articulate a sense of continuity between past and present that was not a grossly ideological construct.

Our discussions revealed the sheer amount of hard work these students had done since 1989 to understand, first, what had happened during the GDR, and then what had happened in Germany during the Nazi period. For the collapse of the communist regime meant the end of the party line that those who had become West Germans were all originally Nazis, while those who had become East Germans had always been heroes of the antifascist resistance. These students had to discover layers upon layers of distortions and untruths. At times it was almost unbearably painful to listen to them as they worked through these layers. When I said, with some hesitation, that Bloch had been executed by the Gestapo in 1944 because he was active in the French Resistance, they grew silent and uncomfortable. They did not speak but wanted to know more about Bloch's life and death. Their silence was not the silence of denial, as it might have been for an older generation. It was the silence that comes from a sense of not knowing enough, of trying to learn more, of needing to understand before speaking. It was a form of tact.

The students could only say so much about what they had experienced in the past and were learning in the present. They needed time, above all, to think through what they were encountering both inside and outside the university.

149

They had experienced too many shocks of recognition in the past eight years or so to speak before long reflection. And yet they showed remarkable resiliency. Perhaps it helped that we were talking about medieval culture rather than twentieth-century history, perhaps it helped that I was American and not West German. Perhaps it helped that I told them my father was Jewish. And perhaps it helped that we spoke in English and not German. For these all gave us ways to think obliquely about what it meant to be meeting as a class four stories above Unter den Linden in June of 1997. That is, of thinking about what it meant to do something that even ten years earlier none of us would have thought possible in the course of our lives.

Platforms in train stations crumbling away, tiles falling off building facades on the former Stalin Allee, decorative stonework of the early twentieth century eaten away by pollution—these are all continual reminders, amid the renovation and construction in Mitte, of the shabbiness that the GDR had become by the late 1980s. Driving through Pankow or elsewhere in the old East Berlin you see bright storefronts at street level with all sorts of attractive objects in the window. And then you look up to the higher floors, which are soot-blackened from the soft coal used to heat buildings. A long accumulation of grit, a lack of materials and money to keep things in repair, hang heavily over these neighborhoods. A few buildings have been repainted, fitted out with new windows, and the difference is startling, in part because these simple improvements make you ask why it had been necessary for people to live in that grayness, that absence of color and light.

The Trabant, the East German car people waited years to buy new and often paid more for used so they could get one sooner, is another visible reminder of life before the *Wende*. Plastic-bodied, powered by a two-stroke engine that belched pollution from the oil and gas mixture it burned, ugly beyond words. Today a Trabant parked in a street beside a modest Volkswagen seems a relic from a time when people heard rumors from elsewhere about things called cars. And from these rumors they cobbled together the Trabant. Crossing rush-hour traffic in Jena, I turned to a friend and said, "However I go, I don't want to be hit by a Trabant." To which he replied, "Not to worry. It would get the worst of any collision."

Nothing in Berlin approaches the desolation one sees from the train as it passes through the old industrial centers of East Germany, such as Leipzig and Bitterfeld. In the aptly named Bitterfeld, once the center of the chemical industry, the factories are empty: windows are blown out, bushes grow through collapsed roofs, the endless pipelines from building to building sag under their own weight. The view speaks of apocalypse, but of a slow variety; it comes not from fire, earthquake, bombing, but from long neglect and final abandonment. Weeds grow in parking lots, strips of paint hang from buildings, the odd piece of rolling stock sits rusting on a railway siding. The leukemia rates here are said to be among the highest in the world.

The signs of desolation in Mitte, such as the pockmarks left behind by bullets and shrapnel fragments, are far more subtle than those in Bitterfeld. Even meticulously renovated buildings can show some of these traces in their stonework if you look carefully enough. More picturesque is the ruin at the edge of the Museum of Natural History: a bombed-out shell from World War II that sprouts grass from its walls and trees from what remains of its roof. It looks like nothing so much as a medieval ruin lovingly tended by caretakers.

Students at the nearby agricultural school of the Humboldt University want it kept in its current state. And it does add a certain charm to the place. As a professor there remarked, with the irony characteristic of the city, it is "the only intact ruin left in Berlin."

This phrase captures that particular moment in Berlin, but it also makes one think about the curious fact that the great museum of Berlin, the Pergamon, has been from the start a collection of intact ruins lifted from various places in the ancient world. This is not just the usual collection of antiquities displayed in cases and halls of sculpture. Here you can see in reassembled form the massive Greek altar from Pergamon in Turkey and the Ishtar Gate from Babylon. Whatever questions of national heritage these ruins raise with respect to their places of origin, they are by now very much a part of twentieth-century Berlin. The history of ruins is a kind of secondary display here, and is the subject of several murals located in the far reaches of the museum, away from the heavy tourist traffic.

These murals, dated and signed "-19-EA-36-," can be found in rooms filled with antiquities excavated from Syria. They depict the sites in idealized form; that is, as ruins that have yet to be dug. A few animals and natives in vaguely appropriate costume appear in each scene but the focus is on the tumulus or mound waiting to be opened. The murals are romantic in style, indulging in an unearned sublimity. They celebrate the workings of time and the wonder provoked by the unspoiled; but their presence in a room filled with artifacts from the site suggests they are meant to celebrate archaeology as the romance of origins and archaeologists as figures of heroic power. If the murals had been painted in the nineteenth century, they would simply seem mythmaking at the expense of the antique past. But painted in 1936, these murals suggest that the ruin is an intact site precisely because it will yield the past one desires. Almost forgotten, these murals may be the most cautionary display in Berlin about the ideological dangers of reading the past.

The fragment keeps one from seeing Berlin as allegory. Details assert the character of the place:

1. In the trainyards of East Berlin, a black, coal-burning steam locomotive fires up next to a white bullet-train;

2. WEST cigarettes, sold in West Germany long before the *Wende*, are advertised with heroin-chic models and an English slogan, "The Power of Now";

3. old Trabants parked on the streets gain new life as movable signs for restaurants and shops;

4. water mains, painted bright colors like pink or yellow or lavender, run twelve to fifteen feet above the sidewalk because the underground lines are unusable;

5. bored riot cops waiting out a demonstration on Unter den Linden pass the time by fixing the windshield wipers on their water-cannon truck;

6. a menu in a trendy restaurant offers Boston spareribs with the promise that they are a traditional American specialty;

7. the globe of the old East German TV tower, called from its shape *Telespargel*, or "TV Asparagus," shows the reflected rays of the setting sun from the west in the form of a Christian cross;

8. a punk pisses openly on Friedrichstrasse and then meticulously places his beer can in a recycling bin;

9. signs on buses and trucks proclaim *Lotto macht Millionäre*; *Wodka Gorbatschow*; *Tour Nostalgie* (on a 1920s-style

bus); *Deutsche Bank; Manhattan Ice Dream, The American Dream of Ice;*

10. the *Tränenpalast,* or "Palace of Tears," where families separated by the division of Germany would say their farewells at the Friedrichstrasse Bahnhof has become a beergarden.

There's a windblown feeling along Leipzigerstrasse where the huge, block-long apartment buildings of 1970s East Berlin stand: lots of scale and an empty monumentality that seem utterly unlike the closed-in feeling of residential neighborhoods from pre–World War II Berlin. Walking past these grandiose buildings, you feel exposed, open to view, without any of the protection that the nooks and crannies of older Berlin give the walker: arcades, courtyards, deeply recessed doorways. It is an unpleasant place to be caught in a sudden downpour. And when I was caught, huddled under the awning of a Chinese restaurant at the corner of Jerusalemerstrasse, the thought came to me that this lack of protection, this exposure to the elements, had everything to do with the politics of the old regime. You were meant to be exposed, to be out in the open without a nook or cranny for shelter. That regime may be gone but an outsider can still sense how it worked by moving through its public spaces.

Now, the shops along Leipzigerstasse have shiny facades and plenty of goods on display: bright clothes, discount electronics, cheerful housewares. McDonalds advertises prominently, and its images of golden arches seem perfectly in place. The only shabby—in fact, only vacant—commercial space for blocks is the *PRAHA* restaurant in what had once been the Czech Center. Its windows are coated with several years of grime and letters are falling out of the old signs. Nobody wants to eat there anymore. Or needs to.

The old proletarian neighborhood evoked in Alfred Döblin's novel of 1929, *Berlin Alexanderplatz*, is long gone. Now it is a vast open space with, at its middle, the "Fountain of Friendship between Peoples." Since the *Wende*, new shops have moved in and neon signs display the names of international business: Mazda, Denon, Fanta, Sanyo, Speedo. On one edge of the platz, across the street, a social-ist-realist mural of noble workers appears in the same view as a huge blue sign for FIAT. Even on a sunny day in June the place makes you think of bleak December afternoons when the sky is gray and the wind blows old newspapers round and round. The empty ceremonial spaces of East Germany, such as the Alexanderplatz, have a brutality that persists despite the change of government and the inrush of capitalist consumerism. Even in rebuilt form, these spaces seem too big.

An interracial church choir from Chicago was visiting when I walked through the square and I could only wonder why this, of all the sights in Berlin, was on their itinerary. Perhaps so they could shop in the electronics store that would have done any American mall proud with its mer-chandise and prices. Perhaps because the guides wanted Americans to see that what had once been East Berlin was fast catching up to Western standards. If so, I hope they walked the Americans past the tight circle of punks hud-dled under a covered walkway at the edge of the place. Against the unrelieved black of their clothes, the only visi-ble color came from the red and white chevrons of their Marlboro packs.

The officially posted text on the fence reads: "Checkpoint Charlie, once the political focal point of the Cold War, now is a construction site for five new buildings and will become a prominent symbol of free trade." One of the buildings has been designed by Philip Johnson, a fascist sympathizer in the 30s. Now, finally, Johnson gets his chance to be a master-builder in Berlin. At this moment, it all comes together: his old politics, his edifice complex, his status as the favorite architect of late international capitalism. On the billboard at Friedrichstrasse 200 he stands smiling and pointing to a rendering of the building still under construction. His image is surrounded by cement mixers and front-end loaders. The building, as it emerges, promises to be utterly clichéd, a box of metal and glass with a few postmodern flourishes that could be anywhere corporations build their headquarters. The architect's major contribution seems to be his name: Philip-Johnson-Haus. Where once the CIA and the Stasi had stared at each other from the upper floors of grimy buildings along the Wall, there will be a new crossing zone for money. The Cold War ends in a farce of postmodern kitsch: Checkpoint Charlie becomes Checkpoint Cash.

About a kilometer north, on the blocks between Unter den Linden and the River Spree, Friedrichstrasse is being completely rebuilt, from sewer lines through to new side-walks. From a certain angle, the construction barriers and heavy equipment that force cars to move at a crawl and constantly shift lanes look like nothing so much as photos of the eastern side of the old Checkpoint Charlie. Bulldozers have replaced tanks, and the danger to anyone crossing comes from an accelerating BMW rather than a border guard's machine gun, but the pattern of traffic flow seems eerily to reenact what once stood blocks to the south on Friedrichstrasse.

Looking at the streets of Berlin means learning to read the reenactment of place: the old patterns that seemed gone forever reemerge in unexpected ways. These patterns reveal and distort at the same time, and thus remind you that all claims about this city and its history must be provisional. To complete the metaphor by making it literal again, the streets are filled with detours and unexpected turnings so that even a one-way street, an *Einbahnstrasse*, will be reversed for a few days so trucks can serve a building site.

Overheard snatches of tourist-guide talk on Unter den Linden make clear that Mitte is a place whose history must be told and retold, to Germans as well as to outsiders. There are buses from elsewhere in Europe along this street, though hardly as many as there would be in a similar area of Paris. Most of them have signs that declare their German provenance. Many are from the more distant states, especially Bavaria. They are so numerous that it can be difficult to photograph a historic site, especially one that has an obvious vantage point that an idling bus can occupy. They pull up, one after the other, while the guides deliver their spiels to the seated tourists, and then move on to the next site. The spot is filled immediately by the next bus in line. On a Thursday morning I waited for over half an hour for the buses to go so I could get a clear photograph of the balcony from which Karl Liebknecht proclaimed the socialist republic in 1918. When the photographs were developed, the image with the buses jammed in front of the balcony was far more evocative than the one I waited so long to take because it showed the site as a public spectacle.

Sitting out a rainshower on a Saturday afternoon under the Brandenburg Gate, I was approached by a young man from Egypt (as he explained) who asked in impeccable English if I knew much about the place. He was dressed in expensive sports gear and carried a shopping bag from Planet Hollywood. He could have been anywhere or from anywhere. When I told him I knew a bit about Berlin, he seemed relieved and quickly asked which was east and which was west. I pointed east and then west. So much for my obsession with history and place.

The voices of history that reverberate across Berlin are most present in the concentration camp at Sachsenhausen, just outside the city. The museum there, built in 1961 by the GDR, still maintains its original display of black-and-white photographs from the old days showing Party leaders laying wreaths and inaugurating the ghastly memorial to the political prisoners who were killed there by the Nazis. At the center of each photograph, or so it seems in memory, are figures of the regime in dark suits and hats; they look prosperous, certain of the role they are playing at this site, convinced. On the edges of these photographs are those who had been political prisoners in Sachsenhausen. Their faces, especially in the older photographs, seem shadowy, difficult to interpret, withdrawn in the midst of the public ceremony they are attending. Accompanying each photo is a neatly typed label in German giving the date it was taken and the names of those it depicts. The Sachsenhausen of these displays is less a museum than a martyrology, a site of unwavering heroism, as is apparent from the socialist-realist images in stained glass that greet you at the museum's entrance and from the memorial of poured concrete at the far end of the camp. The tower of that memorial is unadorned except for the red triangles worn by the political prisoners of the Nazis. This monument remembers no other group of prisoners.

From the photos in the original GDR installation you will not learn that for five years after the war's end the Russians used Sachsenhausen as a prison for their political enemies and then handed it over to the GDR to use for the same purpose. In this installation, Sachsenhausen's history as a concentration camp ceases in 1945 when the Russian army liberated it. Subsequent years go unmarked, just as prisoners who were not political go unnoticed. After the *Wende* another voice was added to the museum's walls to speak— of necessity and by design—alongside that from the GDR period. On long scrolls that hang from the ceiling appears in large bold print the complicated history of the camp in the years before and after 1945. The voices telling this story speak in both German and English. That this revisionist account of Sachsenhausen appears in English gives it authority to reach the larger world.

Nothing in the museum can speak to the desolation of the camp. Most of the barracks are gone, each marked in absence by a large block of stone that bears its number. The exterior walls and guard towers remain, as does some of the barbed wire, rusted and broken into bits. The site is mainly a large grass field, with a few wild flowers of white and blue. On a hot June afternoon the dust blows off the paths.

In the midst of the open ground, a tent stands to document where, in 1992, Neo-Nazis torched several of the surviving barracks that had once held Jewish prisoners. Inside the tent are exhibits of the destroyed barracks because the desire to eradicate history, to burn it off the ground, must itself be remembered. And that becomes another voice in your head as you walk the camp, one that must be included along with those printed on the walls of the museum, and with those that can no longer speak for themselves.

Walking into Sachsenhausen I passed some teenagers photographing each other beside the sign on the gate that reads "ARBEIT MACHT FREI." On leaving, I passed a group of Gypsies coming to mourn their dead. Another voice to hear, to record.

The view from the River Spree, except around Museum Island in Mitte, is not like the view from the Thames or the

Seine. Berlin did not plan its great buildings and public spaces around the river, but inland, because it was a Prussian military city and needed grand avenues and parade grounds to display infantry. Yet from a boat on the Spree you gain an unintended vantage point for seeing the city. Everything becomes disoriented when you look, for example, at the Reichstag from an oblique distance so that, in the foreground, a vast construction site fills the space where the Wall ran to the river.

For most of the run, the trip on the Spree is a pleasant excursion, especially in the west where its banks are heavily wooded and people use the greenspace to stroll, play with kids, escape the pavement of the city. It seemed right that one German couple brought their big dog along on the boat. He slept, they drank beer, all were happy. Part of that happiness came from the fact there is little palpable sense of history visible from the Spree. The Charlottenburg Palace is not, like the Louvre or the Tower of London, built on the river. Only as the boat makes its turn through Mitte and the Museum Island does the city emerge as a place where too much has happened: the Bode and Pergamon Museums, the Prussian Arsenal that is now the historical museum, Humboldt University, the Cathedral, the Palace of the Republic. One senses here that these have always formed the center of the city throughout its various incarnations. To get this coherence you need to return to the streets and move among the buildings. That the city does not derive its plan from the river is proof of its martial character, and modernity.

In Berlin, where the intended view is often too painful to hold for long, it is useful to see from the oblique, from the unintended angle that is opened up by changes of history. Put it this way: the angles of sight in Berlin are those of grand avenues and ceremonial approaches, such as the Brandenburg Gate with its chariot and four horses facing east, the Quadriga. These angles of sight carry with them political impositions. To see otherwise, as from the river, is a relief, an opening into what was not intended or desired. Much the same holds for looking at buildings wrapped in plastic and scaffolding, or for glimpsing the Brandenburg Gate across a construction fence covered with bright posters for a spectacle called "Erotik-Life." At such moments, nothing looks imperial and thus nothing looks as it was meant to look in Berlin.

At the "New Watch," the Käthe Kollwitz statue of a mother holding the dead body of her adult son is low to the ground, heavy, maternal. She is meant to hold all the griefs of this world. Despite its earnestness, its somber dull bronze, this statue of the earth mother stands for nothing so much as the failure of representational art. It wants to rip our guts out, to make us howl for all the sorrows of the century, and thus fails. It lacks the mute eloquence of the memorial to the book-burning across Unter den Linden. The statue looks like nothing so much as a pietà, and sets off questions about what is being remembered and how it is to be remembered. For if this monument does acknowledge, as the sign outside says, victims of the *Konzentrationslager*, then why is the image here so resonant of Christianity? Or, more precisely, of the Christian story about the son who was sacrificed by his father for the redemption of humankind? For what can that say to those who would remember the six million of the Holocaust?

These questions about the statue are ways of saying that there is something more than a little confused about this site. Built originally as a guardhouse for the Prussian emperor's watch in 1818, it became: in 1931, a monument to German troops who fell in World War I; in 1960, a GDR memorial for the victims of fascism and militarism; in 1969, the resting place for an unknown soldier and an unknown camp victim; in 1993, a place of memory as well for civilian victims of Nazism and those who resisted totalitarian dictatorship after 1945. Too many people have put the memorial at the Neue Wache to too many purposes. It bears as a result an impossible name: "Central Memorial of the Federal Republic of Germany for the Victims of War and Tyranny."

Inside the building there is a gloomy solemnity. The floor of irregular, small, dark gray paving stones, the walls, made from blocks of limestone of a lighter gray are subdued, even antimonumental. Above the statue of mother and son is a round skylight that focuses the light on these two figures as if to offer a ray of hope, a beam of illumination; but one knows they cannot be so easily illuminated. Very few visitors descend the two shallow steps from the entrance level to the floor of paving stones, where the statue rests, though that is permitted and some have left flowers at its base. There seems to be a felt need here not to walk too close, not to cross the symbolic space of memory. At such places, even a few feet of distance becomes necessary.

It was better to look through the vertical iron bars that close off the two side entrances because doing so evokes the photographs taken in 1945 during the liberation of the camps. Better to think of the gaunt, skeletal faces that stared out at the photographers from behind the fences, those specters who somehow managed to survive. For then the heaviness of the Kollwitz figures becomes unbearable. Their physical weight, their fleshiness becomes a form of denial. Grief here should be skeletal, gaunt, the last remains of the human body at the edge of extinction. The statue is wrong in another way. In its vision of war, young men suffer actively and die, while their mothers suffer passively and survive, one in battle and the other at home. But the twentieth-century has had no place for such chivalric roles as the valiant fallen son and the nobly grieving mother. To memorialize women with this statue effaces the suffering and death women themselves knew in a time when there were no distinctions between the killing fields and home.

When the books were burned on May 10, 1933, Opern-platz (now Bebelplatz) was a park-like space with trees. Now at the center of its paving stones there is a square of glass, perhaps 1.5 meters square, set flush to the ground. It opens to a view of a larger room below. On each side of this room, which is perhaps 3 meters square, is a tier of ten bookshelves that runs from floor to ceiling. The interior is painted white. All of the shelves are empty. As a German friend said to me wisely, "How else can you memorialize something which has been burned and is no more?" There is a muteness here that seems infinitely moving. Set as it is amid, yet below, the grandiose buildings along Unter den Linden, the starkness of this memorial seems just because it is silent. Two small bronze plaques on either side of the glass square record the event and quote three lines from Heine on the human cost of book-burning. It is a place of sadness.

Now, several years after the memorial was installed, its thick green glass is scuffed and, at certain times of the day, difficult to see through. In the morning, when the sun shines at an angle, you must put it behind you so you can cast a shadow that cuts the glare and lets you look past the glass to the white interior. At no time of the day can you photo-graph through the glass to the room below; you can only photograph those looking at it from above. It is a memorial that rejects the idea of the monumental as publicly visible, as calling attention to itself. From Unter den Linden, per-haps fifty meters away, you will not know it is there, though you may wonder why there are people staring at the paving stones of the platz. The book memorial rejects what looms behind on Unter den Linden, the huge monument of Frederick the Great looking eastward. That statue now seems an unconscious parody of empire's pomp: lots of metal, a big horse, grandly phrased inscriptions. The book memorial sinks below the surface to remember what happened and then what was suppressed. Under the communist regime, the site was a parking lot.

This monument seems complete precisely because it cannot be photographed through its glass and reproduced mechanically. It forces one to look at the site itself and remember it not as image but as the space of a defining historical event. That it denies viewers the conventional gestures of mourning and regret may be grasped from the fact that not once in the month during which I visited it daily did I see a bouquet of flowers laid there. There were bouquets at the Neue Wache across the street, on Frederick the Great's grave at Sans Souci in Potsdam, as well as on his statue on Unter den Linden, among the stones of the bombed-out Frauenkirche in Dresden. But never at Bebelplatz.

A different memorial to the book-burning occurs daily in the front courtyard of the main university building across Unter den Linden. Sellers of used books set up their tables and do a good business with students, faculty, and tourists. From a certain angle, one can look through the book-buyers to see across the street to where, flush to the ground and mute, rests the memorial to the burning of the books. That view of people freely buying and reading books is worth more than all of the bouquets left at the official sites of memory.

As I finish writing these notes about Berlin, I receive a summons for jury duty in federal court in Columbus, Ohio. I arrive at the appointed time but after answering a few questions, I am excused from service because I know too much about this case involving a local Neo-Nazi warlord. Having been convicted of robbing banks to finance his political group, he now faces charges arising from a gunfight with the FBI when he was arrested less than two years ago. Of the 220 people called for jury duty, only 25 or 30 ask to be excused because they have prior knowledge of the case. A past so recent it can only be called the present slips out of memory here in Ohio, and I think again how much harder it must be to remember in a city, like Berlin, filled with monuments and memorials.

Writing Home: High Street

High Street runs through Columbus, Ohio, as a spine. Its character shifts along its length to reflect the surrounding area: the old downtown with government and commercial offices; the rehabbed gallery district; an amorphous university community; quiet residential neighborhoods with wood-frame houses from the early twentieth century. But it remains always the main street of the city, the north-south line that separates cross-streets into east and west, that serves as the origin point for giving directions. High Street is the main axis for Columbus's grid pattern so that, if you can find it, you are never really lost in the central city. Its name comes from those New Englanders who settled this part of the country after the Revolutionary War, and the occasional anglophile will slip in the definite article as if speaking of an English town: The High Street. But that usage seems almost comic because it is not a street of half-timbered houses, pub signs, and hanging flower baskets.

Over the years the foursquare, though rarely distinguished, brick buildings that line the street have suffered

167

more from botched attempts at modernization than outright neglect. Their slapped-on false facades, out-of-date neon signs, unused upper floors all testify in one way or another to their owners' doomed efforts to stem the drift of businesses to the suburbs in the 1950s and 1960s where life was newer and parking easier. Along some stretches, the street has been cut into jaggedly: original buildings were torn down and replaced with one-story strips or supermarkets set far back so shoppers can park in front. This exploitative use of space makes what once had been a symmetrical main street with a trim curbline appear ragged and disconnected. Only in the last several years have zoning regulations been changed to limit setbacks; new buildings must now abut the sidewalk and have their parking lots in the rear, as was the custom in the early 1900s. This return to older practice has become a selling point. A recent for-sale sign on an empty lot along High Street featured a drawing of a typical, early-1900s storefront with signs for imagined businesses that read "Upscale Restaurant" and "Delicious Bakery." A fashionable coffeeshop has just been built on that site with no setback. Even as the building was being finished, it was hard to remember that it was replacing a drive-through beer store that had in turn been a gas station.

The traffic along High Street is steady, sometimes heavy, and always punctuated by buses running north and south. That it has the most regular service in the city, with a bus every seven to ten minutes, is another sign that it is a main drag. In a city that belongs to the car culture of the American heartland, High Street is one of the few places where you will see people walking. Except for several gentrified blocks in the Short North section, with chic restaurants and galleries, much of High Street can still evoke, for those willing to see it, the sense of a small city from early in the twentieth century. But it takes patience to find that city amid the parking lots, the chain drugstores, the fast-food franchises that fill the air with their aromas, the constant flow of traffic that passes along the street without looking at what lines each side.

The few square miles of the world that I know best fall along High Street between Clintonville, the neighborhood of World War I–era houses where I live, and the Ohio State University, where I teach. The distance is about two miles or perhaps forty minutes by foot but I almost never make it in less than an hour because I stop to look in store windows or explore the ways people use the street and its adjacent network of alleys. For ten years or so I have wandered in this neighborhood, buying necessities like food and hardware, spending too much money on used books and cameras, always trying to ease some of the restlessness that comes with a steady life set in one place. Making an alley do the work of the exotic unknown may seem silly, perhaps even pathetic, but it is better for the imagination than reading exploraporn or watching action movies. It gets one out of the house, and that is the first benefit of travel.

Clintonville along High Street is a neighborhood that needs to be walked, not because it is scenic, but because it must be peeled back layer by layer. That way you can see how it has shifted from generation to generation, how it shifts as you walk it day by day. These changes rarely force themselves on you; they can easily be ignored. But paying so little attention to where you live leaves you increasingly unable to appreciate anywhere else, no matter how dramatic. Looked at carefully, though, these two miles of High Street record a changing America. Different moments from the past have left their traces along the street, and they can be read like geological striations or the *pentimento* of an artist's canvas. The painted signs on brick buildings—for long-gone places like Burkart's Economy Stores and a lunchroom called Clinton Villa, or still thriving ones like Schreiner's Hardware and Pace-Hi Beer and Wine Shop—are now so faded as to be barely readable. When they were fresh and garish in their deep colors, these signs must have seemed as arresting as the neon fast-food signs of today. The few that survive along High Street have paled into the brick walls of buildings and no longer catch the eye.

Some of the old back-lit signs that preceded neon remain in place, though the names on them change as tenants come and go. Clintonville Hardware becomes Midwest Photo Exchange, but the sign remains in place. Along this stretch, other buildings have been turned from their original uses as auto showrooms and furniture stores to more improvised purposes, and sheds off of alleys hide old cars soon to be vintage. Nothing here is abandoned in a derelict or wasteful way, nothing here gives cause for fear or even much regret. It's just that people seem to have forgotten to use the upper floors of buildings or the sheds behind them. As life goes on elsewhere, these spaces have lost their purpose.

Wandering around these alleys, down these nooks and crannies, has given density to my life; it has taught me about the uncelebrated persistence of what was built and occupied more than a generation or two ago. I have not lived here long enough to see ghosts turning these corners, nor do I have family ties than run back several generations, as I do in Buffalo. Yet walking these blocks and looking through alleyways behind buildings toward High Street has given me a sense of how the lives passed in a place leave their scars on it. It matters to these wanderings that this is not a "quaint" or "charming" stretch, one gentrified to sterile tastefulness. Instead, it is visibly a mixed-up area with con-

venience stores, insurance agencies, transmission shops, and
a few local bars set beside deeply expert dealers from whom
you can purchase a used Ferrari or Mercedes-Benz, an antique Stickley chair, or a new Leica camera. No one planned
the neighborhood to be this way, no one has yet driven out
the service stores to make room for more boutiques. In an
impromptu way, it simply happened, and in happening
found its comfortably jumbled character.

I began wandering around High Street in a desultory way
at the same time I started writing this book, though I did
not then see any connection between these two parts of my
life. Only after writing the chapter about Berlin, with its
references that brought me back eerily to Buffalo, and then
to Columbus, did I realize this book would have to end with
home. Any other choice would mean evading—in a book
about the power that places have over us—the place that
occupies my life. Home in this sense is not some edenic
place where all sits well with my soul, where I am at one
with the world or where I connect with my past, but where
creditors and relatives know to find me. It is also where,
when I have insomnia, I read travel books. And, as I have
learned over and over again from reading these books, home
is where all is routine and deadening, where everything has
been seen and done countless times. Home seems, in them,
further proof that familiarity breeds contempt.

Or does this vision become fixed because home is the
hardest place to write? It offers none of the easy charge that
comes with travel, that burst of lively impressions and emo-
tive responses that can fill pages. The quick take on elsewhere always gives the travel writer something to work with;
the fact of difference is the easiest subject to exploit, never
mind that it usually turns to shlock. And, besides, home is
the place where you write, the place of work, and thus hardly

likely to be a compelling subject. If, by some lucky chance, you can write about a home place that is wonderfully touristic, then the work is easier because most readers will treat your book as surrogate travel. But what if the home place you write about is neither so alluring nor so appalling as to have some obvious appeal? What if it is neither, to cite clichés, Tuscany nor Siberia?

Thoreau made a necessary point about the mysteries of home when he said in *Walden* that he had traveled a good deal in Concord, but I distrust him because his boasting tone sounds oddly like that of trekkers just back from the Himalayas. And now that Walden Pond has become a pilgrimage site, Thoreau's gibe against travelers sounds self-congratulatory. To think through home, I try instead to puzzle out the case of Cézanne. He found it enough to paint his own native landscape, or his own family and friends, or the household utensils and pieces of fruit on his kitchen table. By doing so, he made it impossible for other painters to look at their world, in all its variety, as they had done for centuries. His work was revelatory because he stayed home. Perhaps painters, who need a lot of gear, learn to be cleverer about what they can find at home than do writers, who travel light. Still, there are writers who, while justly praised for their accounts of foreign places, took home as their great subject and there found the book of their life. V. S. Pritchett is fascinating on Spain, for example, but his *London Perceived* works the magic of making that city seem, beneath its familiar forms, utterly unearthly.

Home, I sometimes think, is where we can most afford to ignore the influence of place. It seems at once familiar and unchangeable, the qualities most likely to make us turn away from a place and think of parts elsewhere. Yet a sense of place is not like a passport, to be pulled out of the drawer only when leaving home. Writing about where you live means describing the same scenes you look at over and over again in the course of days and weeks. Your eyes glaze over, you fail to see, you stubbornly hold to your workaday impressions of the scene. Or you notice only the obvious changes, as when a Shell gas station gets torn down to be replaced by a CVS drugstore, or when another CVS gives way to a Goodwill thrift shop, or when a junky antique shop reopens as Quick Cash USA. But these are superficial changes, minor reweavings of a neighborhood that do not change its texture. To write about home means that you have to look and look again at places, especially those you pass through daily. This work gets shaped through momentary recognitions about things you see frequently but rarely register. It requires as well noticing and telling stories about the people who regularly walk the same stretch of High Street. It means shedding the contempt that comes with familiarity or, even more destructive, its attendant boredom.

By passing a small park at the corner of High Street and Arcadia Avenue, I learned that writing about home needs such momentary recognitions. With its benches and picnic tables, this park fronts on High for perhaps thirty feet, and runs no more than one-hundred deep along Arcadia. It has a sign reading "Welcome to Clintonville" and looks at first glance like one of those green spaces that developers put in when they do not know what else to do with an odd-shaped lot and want to fancy up the area on the cheap. Although it borders on Arcadia, there is nothing pastoral about the park as it sits triangulated amid a White Castle, a Kentucky Fried Chicken, and a Tim Horton's. Depending on the direction of the breeze, you can sit there and smell hamburgers, fried chicken, or donuts. Sometimes, on a day of changeable weather, you get all three. It is the aroma of fast-food

America, and it can make you slightly queasy. Precisely because it is so easy to pass over on the way to elsewhere, this park is a good place from which to watch the neighborhood.

The park always seemed very clean because, as I had assumed when I first walked along High Street, it was never used. I found it convenient to sit on a bench there and scribble notes. As I began to pay attention, I saw that the park had its own population, though perhaps not the one envisioned by its builders. Among them was an old man who used the park as a café on pleasant days; he would elegantly roll a cigarette of Bugler tobacco and sip his cup of White Castle coffee. In another city, this corner would have been ideal for a café because of all the traffic, but here that use had to be improvised by an old-timer at a picnic table. He probably knew what had been on this corner before the fast-food places were thrown up. Perhaps he could have told me whether there was any truth to the stories I had heard about a hobo jungle behind the White Castle in the small ravine that sloped down to the Olentangy River. I did not ask him, though, because the park was finally not a place where one could intrude on the private reveries of a stranger. I was there, it came to me, on his sufferance because I was just passing through and he, as I learned, was something of a regular with his coffee and cigarettes. On sunny days especially I kept an eye out for him, but over time he stopped coming to the park.

The sense that public space like a city park can be intensely private is no paradox. It has everything to do with the ways people use space for their own needs: to be alone, to pass the time, to distance themselves from the flow of life along a main street, to find at times another version of home. In the park at High and Arcadia, I once saw a man of indeterminate age, though certainly not young, sit and read a batch of crumpled pages torn from the Yellow Pages. Far from looking shabby or derelict, he was trim in his immaculate khaki work clothes and Columbus Clippers baseball cap. He read his pages as if they were from a book meant to be gone through from start to finish; he followed the sequence of entries word for word instead of scanning them quickly for a piece of information. He was not looking anything up. He marked nothing with a pen. Was he simply killing time? Had he been laid off? Or retired? He did not look crazy, though his relentless attention to the Yellow Pages disturbed me because he was reading them as no one was ever meant to do. But that, finally, was none of my business because he was not bothering me or anyone else in the park. My mistake was to think of it as a public place.

I have never quite shaken the feeling that this man in his khakis and ballcap, that familiar midwest style for the urban working man, was reading those pages as if to fix the contents of the city forever in his mind. That this knowledge would have been shaped by an arbitrary alphabet, rather than a geographic plan, was his way to find his place and read it as home. The city he made from those listings of addresses and telephone numbers and slogans was as invisible to me as are the cities that Marco Polo invents for Kublai Khan in Italo Calvino's *Invisible City*. My stranger's invisible city was based on the commercial categories of the Yellow Pages. Perhaps, and I open them randomly because I never saw which pages he clutched in his hand, they belonged to a city of: Bags-Plastic, Bail Bonds, Bakers' Equipment, Bakers-Retail, Bakers' Supplies, Bakers-Wholesale, Balancing Service-Industrial, Baling Supplies and Equipment, Balloons-Decorators, Balloons-Hot and Cold Air, Balloons-Novelty and Toy-Retail, Ballrooms, Bands and Orchestras, Bank Equipment and Supplies, Bankruptcy Services, Banks-Com-

175

mercial and Savings, and on and on through the letter *B* to Butchers' Equipment and Supplies, Buttons-Advertising, and Buttons-Clothing. From such categories, he could have created a story for his city.

However he might have told his city, I can write these two miles of High Street only through the passing of time, through the ways it holds the history of the place. For that reason, my most treasured encounter along this stretch of High Street was one I had with a sporty gent straight out of Damon Runyan's stories for *Guys and Dolls*. He was wearing a dark suit and shirt, jazzy tie, cloth cap. He was standing at the stop as if the bus would, when it picked him up, take him straight to the track, where he could place a few two-dollar bets on his favorite ponies and chat up some of the good-looking railbirds. And if the world were a better place, the bus would have done just that. As I walked by, looking far from jaunty on my way to work, he greeted me, a total stranger, "Good morning, sir. It is a desirable morning." To which I could only add, "It certainly is." Now, looking back, I wish I had skipped school and spent the day wandering around Columbus with him and asking him for his memories of the place when he was young and sports wore fedoras and smoked cigarettes without filters and carried *The Racing Form*.

Meetings between strangers along this stretch of High Street are rare. Mostly they are the predictable exchanges of a quick hello or a polite request for directions. Typical was one I had with a young man wearing the international uniform of jeans and Nikes and backpack. He stopped to ask me on which side of High Street he would find the bus for Ohio State. In its various ways—where was the bus? in which direction was the best-known landmark in the city?—this question marked him as a stranger, as did his limited but very correct English. From his accent, he seemed most likely a native speaker of Arabic. I guessed he had just begun taking classes in English as a Second Language at the old North High School, a block up Arcadia. This moment of giving directions made the park at High and Arcadia into an urban space where anyone could meet. That the neighborhood high school was now used for teaching immigrants and others who were not the usual teenagers of the neighborhood showed how the city's population had changed over the last generation or so. And that could also be seen by anyone who read the signs for the restaurants and food stores along my two-mile stretch of High Street.

This new history for High Street can be measured by three Asian groceries in the space of six blocks, an Indian grocery and, most of all, by the Mediterranean market that stocks goods from Spain, through the Middle East, and then beyond to India. The owners of this store, a family of Lebanese, have the weary dignity that comes from living in and then leaving a hard part of the world. They remember your preferences in olives or feta cheese, they exchange recipes and greetings of the season, but you know that they refrain from telling you the story of their lives because that would be too alien for the heart of the midwest. And yet, as you walk this part of High Street, you can see traces of many other people who have left their home countries to settle here. The restaurants and their names tell various versions of that story: several Chinese places, including an all-you-can-eat buffet that does an enormous business at lunch, Aladdin's, Sinbad's, Blue Nile Ethiopian, Indian Kitchen, Alana's, Casa di Pasta, Japanese Oriental Restaurant, Taj Mahal Indian and Pakistani Cuisine, as well as a Korean place that has had several names and the ghost of a Jamaican-Caribbean place that failed. A carry-out store just north of the university had for a time a handwritten sign, amid the beer ads in the window, that read simply: "Call India, 0.59¢ a minute." In the midst of my reveries about the past generations that had once filled these buildings along High Street, a new generation has come to make them its own, to add new smells to the street, to use new words on its signage.

For a few years license plates in Ohio bore the slogan "The heart of it all" to express the state's geographical location in the midwest and its approximate shape. At the center of Ohio is Columbus. Seen from a distance on the interstate, it looks like the archetypal midwestern city on a small scale: the compact skyline with a few tall buildings that mark out the idea of downtown without being one; the acres of single-family neighborhoods with good trees and dull houses that spread farther and farther each year; a ring-road that once circumscribed the outer limits of the city but has now been leapt over by these new developments. Every fast-food place known to the average American, and some yet to be known, can be found in Columbus because the city is a test market for new franchises. The city gave America and the world White Castle, with its original porcelain-clad and crenellated stores; local custom makes it the place to stop for hamburgers and coffee after a hard night of drinking. Wendy's also began in Columbus, but it is a wholesome family place with its freckled and pig-tailed namesake, the idealized fast-food of central Ohio.

That the stretch of High Street I walk should be set in the center of such a state seems at first surprising but then almost inevitable. For Clintonville has become something of a haven for those who resist assimilating into the heart of it all. Local folklore has it that Clintonville—43202 to the U.S. Postal Service—has the highest percentage per capita of lesbians of any zip code in the country. Whether that claim is statistically correct hardly matters because it captures a truth about the neighborhood. Nearer to the university, many undergraduates live in houses that elsewhere would be considered slums, though here they seem a bit less depressing because the students are only passing through for a few years. And they do give the area a sense of noise and energy, sometimes to the point of occasional dumpster fires and confrontations with the police. But this part of the neighborhood feels like others in almost any American college town.

The character of the neighborhood is defined more particularly by a quiet and even decorous distance from mainstream culture, so that in local restaurants like Hound Dog Pizza and Whole World Natural Foods you can see old counterculture types and Gen-Xers at neighboring tables. Two generations, distant enough to be parents and children, coexist with a certain tolerance and a shared fondness for fetish objects like the retro-look Volkswagen Beetle. If I were to learn, sitting among these tables, that some Weathermen or other 1960s radicals had gone underground in this neighborhood with false identities, I would not be surprised. They would have found fellow spirits on these quiet streets, people whose books and posters and records would have made a common bond without any need for explanation. Hound Dog gently teases the neighborhood style by proclaiming "Pizza for the People" and by delivering in a red Volkswagen with a toy rocket, surmounted by a plastic hound dog, on its roof. When the place opened, it used an aging red Cadillac for the rocket and hound but then it got junked. I still miss that piece of automotive bizarrerie cruising joyfully up and down High Street. Even on the grayest day it made me laugh at its brilliant recycling of an old luxury sedan.

The first clue I had to the neighborhood's character came, shortly after I moved there, when I went to visit Phoenix Books. I had assumed it was a used-book store with a witty name: old books brought back from the ashes for a second life like the marvelous bird of regeneration. It was, I quickly discovered, about a different kind of regeneration, because it turned out to be a New Age shop selling books, pamphlets, candles, and crystals with the promise of metaphysical and mystical knowledge. For a time, another such store, Pearls of Wisdom, was a few blocks away, until it moved to a much larger space to accommodate its many customers. A similar place, closer to the university, has a barely visible sign that reads Fly-by-Night Magical Resource Center. I've never gone in because no place could fulfill the promise of that name and, besides, how could it keep regular business hours?

For a year or so, while both lasted, I defined the neighborhood by two adjoining stores near where I live: "Arjuna Movement Arts / Yoga and Tai Chi" and "Paragon Boutique / Angels." On sunny afternoons, the owner of Paragon would stand outside dressed in full, white angel regalia and wave to passing drivers who would, in turn, honk their horns in greeting. It seemed almost sacrilegious to make such noise, but how else were you to greet an angel, especially one of considerable, earthbound bulk? She had a large sign in front of her store that seemed about as Christian as the neighborhood could tolerate: "One God / One Judge / Love / Your / Neighbor." When her store folded, the space was taken over by the people next door, suggesting that movement arts are more profitable than spirituality. And then in time the storefront passed to a used furniture store called Retro Metro run by people too young to remember much from before 1975. The last time I walked by, it seemed empty and about to post signs announcing a big sale.

Retail outlets specializing in mystical knowledge seem all the more visible along this strip of High Street because it has only one traditional place of worship, the Clinton Heights Lutheran Church, built in the early 1960s. There are other churches set a block or so back from High on residential streets, but as far as the surviving buildings indicate, there have never been many churches along it. Other main streets in Columbus have plenty of churches, so their absence on my walk puzzles me. Perhaps it has to do with the ways the neighborhood defined itself, with businesses on High Street and churches and homes on the side streets, a kind of distinction between public commerce and private life. For an outsider this means that you have to search for a church; for a resident it means there is a comfortably seamless flow between where you live and worship. That churches are usually surrounded by houses is another way in which the area resembles a village. But there is no point in getting sentimental about this quality. Several years ago, the one church on High Street bought and tore down the perfectly livable house behind it to gain parking for another twenty-five cars. The church should have put up a sign saying "Parking before People" to counter the "People before Profits" bumper sticker popular in the neighborhood.

Amid the New Age fuzziness of angels and alternative forms of knowing, the hard facts of life get registered on High Street by two prosperous funeral homes. Each occupies a replica plantation mansion, as if the dead are best sent heavenward from this mortal coil through Tara. But these buildings fade into movie-set décor beside a nondescript, two-story, beige-brick building with a sign outside stating "Capital Care Women's Center." No one is fooled by that neutral title. Both the clients who go inside and the protestors who remain outside know it is an abortion clinic.

And here the gently decorous tone of the neighborhood changes. Often there are picketers, keeping their mandatory distance from the clinic's door, but still displaying gestures of fanaticism. From time to time, a young woman walks the sidewalk with her anti-abortion placard. On the trunk of her car, she displays a series of plastic models showing the developmental stages from egg and sperm to nine-month-old fetus to deter woman from entering the clinic. More often the protestors are men in their twenties and thirties. One wears a ball cap emblazoned "Jesus," a large wooden pectoral cross, and a medallion of the Virgin Mary. The most regular of the group, a gaunt figure who has come to fascinate me, paces up and down in a private reverie of motion, counting out his rosary as he goes. I have never heard him speak to anyone walking down the street or going into the clinic. He is oblivious to people, conversing only with his God. He has the familiar face that haunts you from the edge of a religious scene, the face of the true believer that lives on the intensity of his faith. He looks ready to pose for a Spanish portrait of a religious ecstatic searching for martyrdom. Among the vapid local purveyors of the mystical arts, he is a reminder that religion has always been about life and death, not self-knowledge.

Watching this man, more a character from an auto-da-fé than a local resident, gets at the juxtapositions that define life along a major city street. Some of these are unintentionally humorous, like the do-it-yourself carwash, the oil-change place and the Mexican restaurant that all occupy the same building. But most of these neighborhood juxtapositions seem grimmer. Across High Street from the plasma center is a liquor store where people cash the checks they get for selling their blood to then buy alcohol. The two businesses exist in liquid symbiosis, a relation of necessity in a world of poverty and addiction, despair on display as people cross the street between them. There are other reminders of mortality that make me shudder whenever I see them. Most sobering of all is a shop window displaying the appliances of aging and infirmity: wheelchairs, crutches, walkers with wheels and hand-brakes, hospital beds, bed pans, bed wedges, and other objects too mysterious to identify. I fear these objects as I fear little else I see daily, exactly because they are about immobility, about not being able to wander freely from place to place. I try, when I can, to walk this block on the opposite side of the street so I can evade this store or, at least, enjoy looking across at its incongruous proximity to a health-food store. Looking for irony is the walker's defense as much as the reader's.

City life lies in these incongruities. Urban planners can never achieve these effects, these moments of pathos or humor, because they believe in regularity and permanence. The design for a cityscape is to be built and fixed in place. Or, if it changes, it must be approved by a review board charged with maintaining standards, which means maintaining sameness. But the city spaces we move through are always changing, always reminding us that we use place in necessarily impermanent ways. High Street along these two miles belongs to a city because here things meet that planners would have us keep apart or hidden. The ugly business of selling blood for alcohol is not part of anyone's ideal city, and hiding it away would only make it easier to pretend that it does not exist. Keep it on the main drag, and then perhaps we can face what it tells us about the lives other people lead around us.

Other incongruities register on the signs that clutter High Street. Some are amusing, like the icy-blue neon sign for "Fate Tattoos" that looks surgical in its sterility, not at all evocative of ink under the skin. The local Irish bar, Patrick J's, one day had a message on its signboard that read with surprising crudeness for a friendly place: "BIG ASS BEER / HALF ASS PRICE." A few blocks south, "The One and Only Dick's Den," home of jazz music, has a tantalizing sign that asks enigmatically "Why Not?" More difficult to treat simply as incongruity was the large billboard with an image of Jesus Christ that loomed about High Street near the Capital Care Women's Center: "The Greater the Sinner ... / The Greater the right / he has to My Mercy / Pray to End Abortion." Seeing that sign for months on end put one on edge— would it provoke the kind of violence that had led to murders at other abortion clinics in America? Would it be the incitement that drove the religious ecstatic I saw pacing the sidewalk to violence? But that billboard at least had a kind of tactical purpose on High Street. It was meant to intimidate. More bizarre was the billboard that showed on its left side a voluptuous blonde in a bikini and on its right a male beer-belly in profile as it gaped out between a too-small T-shirt and drooping pair of jeans. In between these images, it read: "I hate men's guts" in huge type and then in somewhat smaller type: "Don't be a whopper. / Go vegetarian. / PETA www.MeatStinks.com." The first time I saw that sign from a distance, before I realized it was paid for by People for the Ethical Treatment of Animals, I wondered why anyone would bother to post such a message. The many lesbians who make their home in Clintonville tend to be civil, if not friendly, so that hardly seemed possible as the source for this message. I still, several years after it was taken down, wonder about the message of that billboard; that is, its reason for appearing with that imagery in this neighborhood. Its incongruity, I realized later, was that it was placed a block from the best vegetarian restaurant in Columbus.

That little has been planned along these two miles of High Street has made for some losses—buildings torn down so rows of stores with in-front parking could be put up—but also for some gains, as stores cluster together. The three Asian groceries within six blocks, the antique shops ranging from "early attic" to classic that crowd each other, these and other clusters would never be planned because in a rational economy they would be too close to each other to survive. Yet it is through these violations of rational economy that a neighborhood gains its idiosyncratic and endearing qualities. The three Asian groceries are especially incongruous, for Clintonville is only lightly populated by Asians. But as these stores bring people into the neighborhood to shop, they also break down the lines of orderly planning, the cross-hatchings of grid-plan cities. They make us move beyond our neighborhoods. These small instances of the unexpected redeem our lives from the routine they otherwise follow.

High Street along these two miles is a cityscape adapting itself to changes in the larger area beyond. Viewed in a certain light, for a few blocks, High Street looks as cities did before there were suburbs; and then for other blocks, it has become the suburbs. Most of the people who move through this cityscape do so in cars, but that cannot obscure the street's pedestrian quality, even its similarity to main streets in many Ohio towns. The scale of the street and the original buildings, as well as of the two-story frame houses that are visible on the side-streets, all evoke the late nineteenth and early twentieth centuries. So do the dates on building cornices: 1891, 1892, 1916. The most visible signs of the current moment are the fast-food restaurants and gas stations that run along this stretch of High Street. They are cheap and ephemeral, built for a decade not a century. No one would think to put a date on them. The small electrical

substation on Arcadia just off High looks monumental beside the facades of these fast-food places; its high, arched
window seems elegant in its purpose and endurance. The
substation fills its tiny plot of land with unobtrusive authority. The restaurants, designed so cars can easily park or move
through drive-up windows, seem too small for their lots. The
streetscape in such places becomes diminished, porous, in-
substantial; it bleeds back from the curb-line without defi-
nition. Covered by too much asphalt, these sites seem wasteful rather than expansive in their use of land. The eye asks
what was there once or what will come in a few years; it
never pays much attention to the current scene.

The law of the streets is that one's sense of space is deter-
mined by the distance between the front of a building and
the curb. Or, in simpler terms, does it abut the sidewalk? Is
there a setback for parking? The deeper the setback, the
emptier the space. That emptiness along High Street can at
times be desolate, though it never seems so in front of the
older buildings. The new ones, too far removed from the
street, appear forlorn when no cars are parked in front of
them. After business hours, they look abandoned. Buildings
along the sidewalk never have that feel; after hours, they
simply seem closed for the night. Walk the street often
enough and you will come to think that most of America's
cityscapes, especially in newer suburban areas, are built as
they are because Americans can't be trusted to park in back.

The emptiness along High Street is most haunting where
a gas station between North and Dodridge sits on a full city
block. In the center of this space is a hut for soft drinks and
snacks; it is flanked by gas pumps covered with a large roof
supported on thin pillars. There are no walls, no bounding
of the usable space. It has a flow-through transparency designed for automobiles. It exists to fuel the incessant move-

ment of our lives, the continual driving up and down High Street. There is nowhere along this stretch that is easier to move through in a car, nor any place that would be easier to turn into something utterly different overnight. This kind of building can be found throughout the United States because it does its job well. But no other kind of building seems so much a statement of impermanence. Where the early twentieth-century buildings are intact, the space along High Street is, by contrast, more defined and the light more focused so that the shading across the facades changes during the day. The gas station at High and Dodridge always looks as if it is lit by under-wattage fluorescent tubes.

Walking along High Street, you learn that the relation between buildings and light changes from block to block. Where the alleys survive, there is a greater feeling of density along the street. From them, the street gets its thickness and complexity because the garbage cans, dumpsters, and closed-up garages can be found there. Walking this street, thinking about how buildings fill space and are lit at different times of the day and year is another way to acknowledge the familiarity of place. Responding to patterns of light, to the ways and times it swells to luminosity or fades to shade, is to know a place over a long duration. It is to have the place in one's body. This play of light on one's home ground is the pleasure that comes with living in a place for years.

Most people find this stretch of High Street to be unremarkable, even forgettable. So I wonder if, as a forced exercise in writing, I have made it seem more quirky than it would appear to the average observer. But ten years of wandering around any place should yield at least a few ideas and notes, should make one hesitate to use words like "boring" or "featureless." And it certainly means that one cannot be objective in the ways urban planners and geographers must be. Travelers often describe landscapes as featureless because nothing in them catches their eye. Passing through such places feels like killing time: watching the scene, watching the clock, watching for something to appear. If killing time is a sign of ennui, so is killing place. More exactly, killing place is a sign of the boredom that always needs new sights, that cannot return to a place to look at it again. Its motto is "Been there. Done that." Home can never be its subject.

Day in and day out, the going between home and work seems to define empty movement: infinitely repeated, never changing, without possibility of discovery. Travel, its antidote, is about the continual encounter with the new, about the charge of eros and invention. Beneath the glamour it cultivates so assiduously, however, most travel writing is a deliberate exercise in killing place. To satisfy their readers' desire for the new, travel writers must often forget ruthlessly where they have been before. Writing about home is instead an act of retracing the familiar routes. It is about stopping to look again, not about burning fuel to get out. It is about making sense of all the other places dreamed about and visited. It is about recognizing that the boredom is internal rather than external, in oneself and not some too-familiar place.

Writing about home has its own seductions, its own temptations to honesty. Stories of family betrayal or abuse, of the tyranny and banality that fill life at home: these are the eternal tales from Greek tragedies about aristocrats in Mycenae to the latest memoir of small-town incest in America. These stories are set at home, they take their energy from being there, but strangely they are not about home as a place on the map, as a setting distinct from other places. The stories that home prompts are achingly familiar because they

188

can be located anywhere. They are about family, and that is something apart from our stories of where we live. Crossing an inland sea has led me by an unforeseen route to a midwestern city, and a wood-frame house built in 1917. I write there in a room with a sloping roof and five windows overlooking the street. My walls are covered with maps and prints of places I have written about—Buffalo, Paris, Oklahoma, Berlin—or someday want to know: Patagonia, the route of Odysseus across the Mediterranean. Once I leave my house and these images, it takes me five minutes to walk to High Street. I add these details of placement because my account of Columbus should not be read as an exercise in killing place. Nor is it an exercise in celebrating the charms of the domestic.

If one resists the meretricious glamour of travel writing, one must also resist tempting evocations of home. Having read all of those travel books during insomniac nights, and works of local description as well, I keep remembering a throwaway sentence in one of Albert Camus's notebooks: "After all, we need a native soil and we need travel." Having both means we can escape the false binary of here and there, of mundane and exotic. It means we do not have to reject home as a subject. Yet in our migratory, dislocated time, home is rarely the same place as our native soil. I might call Buffalo my native soil but that seems too incongruous, even portentous, for my experience there. I lived in Buffalo for a time because my mother was raised there, and returned because her parents had settled there as emigrants. My connection to Buffalo runs back almost a hundred years, but by now the city is for me more memory than native soil. Yet as this connection grows thinner over the years, I cannot reject the place. I now live elsewhere, and I must over time make sense of this other place. That process of making sense is the imperative of any place, and it does not demand complete fidelity to one's native soil.

Looking at a place slowly over the years, looking without the vulgarity of purpose needed while traveling, is a hard discipline that seems always to get harder as the scene at home becomes more familiar. For with that familiarity comes an easy certainty about what is there and what is not. Does it make any difference that the junky antique store becomes a check-cashing place if neither touches my life? Such changes can feel at times like the detritus of a too-busy life. But some morning as I am out walking I realize that other changes have crept in and have caught me by surprise. The landmarks have shifted on my home ground and I feel a slight sense of dislocation. I am no longer quite at home and that can be exhilarating.

On one such morning, while revising these pages, I saw that the local real estate office had been stripped of its forty-year-old facade, complete with ersatz shingled roof. It was a place where I always stopped on my walk down High Street because it had a talking window where one could learn details about houses for sale. Press a button, hear about a house. It reminded me of the science museums of my youth. And then its skin had been peeled off to reveal a building still garish in its fresh orange paint with blue lettering that read "Muffler King." It advertised new seat-covers for $11.95, "chrome tips" for exhaust pipes, and brake jobs for $9.95 as long as you drove a 1951–58 Ford or Chevrolet. It was a glimpse into the television version of post–World War II America, a perfectly preserved service station of a sort that had faded from the landscape in the 1960s and 1970s when people started pumping their own gas and going to national franchise places to get their mufflers replaced. When I photographed it I had the feeling of being an industrial archaeologist. Then, a day later, the place was surrounded by chainlink fence and the construction crews were busy throwing another new facade on the building. But these few days of bright orange paint and prices from my childhood made me intensely happy because they proved what I had always thought while walking along High Street: that there were many layers left to peel back, many old signs to discover, many elegies yet to be sung.

Beyond the shape of buildings that line High Street, it is the changing light of home that measures the passing of time for me. The sun fading in the late afternoon across the brick buildings gives me peace because it evokes what has passed and also what might be. Elegy registers what has passed, of course, but always with the hope that someday there will be someone there to hear its song against forgetting. The old poets of Rome and Germania loved to lament the passing of old days by evoking the persistence of places: shattered or diminished as these places may have been, they still survived, if only as names on a map or in a passing mention by a writer. The poets of Anglo-Saxon England comprehended the past through the remains of stone-built Roman buildings—what they called the "old work of giants"—because they themselves lived in a world that built with wood and thus was impermanent. Their elegy for these stone and masonry places was a gesture against forgetting.

The opposing vision to what I feel along High Street is evoked by the Nature Conservancy's list of "The Last Great Places," such as Komodo National Park in Indonesia or the Calakmul Biosphere Reserve in Mexico. These are all sites that must be preserved, I know, but thinking too much about them is a kind of fetish that lets us toss aside as disposable all that does not register as "great" or, more guilt-provoking, as "last." The alleys I walk are not great places, though perhaps they are endangered. No glossy magazine would print my photographs of them or of the changes I describe along High Street. Yet a reverence for place must begin, like charity, at home. Looking at the familiar places of our lives with some saving trace of wonder, and some regard for the lives that were passed there before us, might help us preserve those places designated as great.

High Street is the place I live, the place I see daily. As I drive and walk along it, its story is always changing, always under construction. The gaps along its two-mile stretch and sudden in-fills when a new building appears, its shifting play of light across familiar facades—all of this marks it out as home. My sense of High Street is different from my view of other places because I see it every day and not, as with the others, at punctuated intervals. I write it with an elegiac tone partly to acknowledge its losses but also to celebrate some trace of memory that might be seen in the future. Like all elegies, this is an essay at remembering. It sounds a blue note for what has been passed over, for what has gone unnoticed by those who will not linger to look and look again. It is about the sweet patience that makes place a part of one's life.

Writing in Place

Writing about places one has known well means renouncing all that makes travel glamorous when we read about it: the encounter with the new that holds out the promise of escape, of becoming something more than the product of one's native ground. Travel is alluring because it suggests there is somewhere out there that will yield to our desires.

My way to think about places has been instead to ask how they shape and reshape a life. Sometimes this process comes as a first impression, a snapshot taken through a moving window. By some counts, generations must pass before one becomes rooted in a place; but by others, it may take only a moment to know that a place is where one must live, if only in the imagination. Sometimes this glance through a moving window becomes a promise to immerse yourself in a place, to live there and learn its stories. It honors the work that comes with the rituals and routines of a place: shopping for food, cooking, doing laundry, finding routes between where you sleep and work. This sense of being in place belongs to the time we have on the earth. By contrast, most travelers write as if days spent on the road will not be charged against their allotted span. That is why their books often seem so jaunty.

Against the damage worked by time there is something reassuring about memories of place. Stories told in time move toward death or transcendence; stories told in place shape the settings of our lives. If time is the element we fear because it is inexorable and diminishing, place can be the counterweight for the stories of our lives. Places are, of course, subject to time. One way to sense the damage of the years is through what has happened to places. But places, or more exactly, the senses we acquire of them throughout our lives, give a shape to experience that does not end inevitably in death or transcendence, those overdetermined ends of chronology.

Personal accounts in this book appear only as they are necessary for tracing a larger geography of experience. These encounters with place come from my life but they are hardly unique to it. Reflecting on places, in their variety, is a way of moving away from time, of finding another course to trace the shape of a life. The phrase "from place to place" is beautiful because its narrative rhythm evades the closing of years. So too, the first account of the modern self, Saint Augustine's *Confessions*, is, among many other stories, an atlas of the Mediterranean, of voyages back and forth between North Africa and Italy.

Time filters the tonalities of a scene, heightens the contrasts, diffuses the harsh clarity of memory, and yet the place remains visible and recognized. This metaphor of the filter comes from photography and that matters because much of how we know a place—even one we know from living there—comes through the isolating power of the still photograph. The landscape set at a moment in its natural cycle;

194

the building given structure by a precise detail; the sharp and revealing juxtaposition of familiar and unfamiliar: all of these are absorbed through photographs and have themselves become ways of seeing the places that have inhabited me. If there are some general conclusions to be drawn from these details, they must remain true to the particularity of places as different as Buffalo and Paris, Oklahoma and Berlin, Wyoming and Chartres.

The redeeming wonder of places lies in their confusions. Whether time is circular or linear, it has a pattern of repetition or unfolding. Places have their measures of time, and their history; but past, present, and future can render a site's story only if they run together and deny each other's unique claim to authority. Time matters to places and our sense of them, but as a minor muse rather than governing spirit. When we arrange a set of overlapping maps to depict the history of a city, for example, we are watching it expand or contract across space. But maps are hard to read, as every lost stranger knows, and tell us little about what we will find when we arrive at where we want to be.

Sometimes we find—and this can never be fixed on a map—what we have already read about or seen before we set off. Much of what I tell about a place has been refracted through the experience of viewing images or reading fiction, history, travel accounts. They are the belated legacy of a place. Seeing by means of books and pictures is not a surrogate form of experience, a faded version of some allegedly authentic experience. To think that such an unmediated encounter with place is possible verges on the naive or arrogant. It means, either way, losing the richness of stories and images that gather about a place, that may even be said to *be* the place.

Elias Canetti calls a section of his memoir "History and Melancholy" and much of my writing might be held in place by that phrase. This idea of history and melancholy should not, however, be confused with nostalgia, the easy tone of the travel writer that says places have changed for the worse, that everyone has gotten there too late. The melancholy I feel when writing about places carries a measure of loss but also the weight of too much history, of too many stories. You can complain about how a place fell apart or got ruined or turned boring, or else you can ask how it is that a place happened to get to where it is as you look at it. A sense of history matters for thinking about places. Even in landscapes, with their patterns of earth and water, cloud and light, there is that history. Writers who speak of unspoiled landscape are usually oblivious to the human traces that can be seen on it by those who know it well. The shaping of a landscape by migration routes or settlement patterns is the work of history.

As they circulate, stories create a place; they give it an identity more lasting than any set of coordinates on a map. One has only to set an atlas from 1950 beside one from 2000 to see how dated maps can become in a generation or two. In fact, before there were visual maps of the sort we use daily, there were narrative maps. It was the chain of names and stories that got readers and travelers from place to place, and that taught them about each one along the way. In the narrative geographies of the ancient and medieval West, travel meant learning stories far more often than it meant gaining personal experience. So true could this be that some of the best medieval travel writers, like the fourteenth-century one who called himself Sir John Mandeville, seem never to have left home. Stories came to them instead.

Much as I admire the distant imaginings of a writer like Mandeville, I cannot write from the library and then claim, as he did, that the stories I found there came from my personal travels. But I do envy him his certainty that the best tradegoods from faraway are stories about other places. And I have written my stories of place in that spirit.

Acknowledgments

This book owes much to the people who live in the places I have written about and who have shared their local knowledge with me. My travels with Morris Foster and Joan Cuccio began in Oklahoma but have extended to many other places, including a memorable trip to Orkney. They have been good friends, wonderful traveling companions, and rigorous readers of my prose. Others in Oklahoma helped me learn the place, and for that I thank particularly George D. Economou, Ashley Hall, and June Hobbs.

My experience of Paris owes a great deal to Laura Kleege, who shared her love of the city, her hospitality, and her own life there with extraordinary generosity at a time when I had no more than my own bookish impressions. It saddens me that she did not live to read this book in her apartment on Rue Rollin. Etel Adnan and Simone Fattal also belong deeply to my sense of Paris, to walks in the Left Bank and lovely dinners on Rue Madame.

In Berlin, Ursula Schaefer was a learned and thoughtful guide through the mysteries of that city. Much of what I

199

came to understand about life there came from the long conversations we had when I visited the Humboldt University at her invitation. Most of those who taught me about Buffalo, both family and friends, are now dead, but I remember them all with fondness and admiration for the lives they made in that city on an inland sea. More happily, I thank my sister Nina Howe and my brother-in-law Bill Bukowski for their memories of Buffalo. They remember a different place than I do, as is only to be expected, but they have been firm in their belief that I was correct to begin this book with Buffalo.

Along the way, I have been blessed with wonderful readers and editors. To have had three editors as welcoming as J. D. McClatchy at the *Yale Review*, Michael Walzer at *Dissent*, and Willard Speigelman at the *Southwest Review* seems beyond good fortune. I am pleased to acknowledge their kindness in publishing my writing about places over the last ten years or so. Other friends have read all or parts of this book with care: Charles Berger, David Bromwich, Dick Davis, Carole Fink, Leigh Gilmore, Rebecca Haidt, John Hollander, Nicolaus Mills, Gerald Vizenor, and Andrew Welsh. To Melanie Rae Thon I owe, among other debts, the idea for my title. Roberta Frank has a special place in this book for always telling me that writing it would be good for my work as a medievalist.

The members of the Center for Medieval and Renaissance Studies at the Ohio State University have been wonderfully tolerant about my interest in places far removed from the middle ages. To Suzanne Childs, especially, I owe many thanks for her great good cheer and for her gift of friendship. I count my association with CMRS to be the happiest of my working life.

Mary Murrell at Princeton University Press has been not just an astute and tough editor, with an eye for where the prose goes flat; she has also been something like the ideal reader for this book. I will always remember with great pleasure the e-mail she sent me in October 2001 asking about the book on places I claimed to be writing. I thank as well the two readers for the Princeton University Press who wrote reports that helped me better understand my book and guided me through revisions. Jonathan Munk copyedited the manuscript with a sharp eye and a deft touch.

My friends Stu Applebaum and Abdi Roble of the Midwest Photo Exchange in Columbus have patiently given advice about cameras, lenses, and film that saved me from many mistakes. I am especially grateful to Stu for always asking me what I was writing and thus reminding me, when I would rather have talked photography, that I needed to go home and sit at my desk.

My late parents, Thalia Phillies Feldman and Irving Howe, read the earliest sections of this book, and encouraged me to continue with it. I hope they realized, as they read those pages, that they were responsible for starting me on the subject of place by taking me to Greece in 1957 and then again in 1958. Ilana Wiener Howe has kept at me to finish this book, and has always been happy to talk about books and places. For her encouragement, her faith, and the use of a beautiful house in which to write, I am as always grateful to Arien Mack.

Many strangers, people I met and talked with in the places I was visiting, have left their mark on this book. I wish it were possible to thank them all by name, but in lieu of that I acknowledge a few: the old sport on High Street, the young Egyptian at the Brandenburg Gate, the gas station attendant in Hyannis, Nebraska, and the children in the cemetery in Hugo, Oklahoma. The kindness of strangers who offered directions, restaurant suggestions, historical information, or simply shared their love of places with me is everywhere present in this book.

The dedication to Georgina Kleege honors a shared life of almost twenty-five years. She has been the best of readers, the most stalwart of supporters. She has also been a great road warrior, accompanying me to places that were sometimes far distant from her own beloved places. Most of all, she has taught me by her own example the saving grace of good prose.

Notes

I have limited these notes to the acknowledgment of direct quotations and specific sources of information cited in my text. Many other books have shaped the ways I have seen and written about places, but they are far too numerous to mention individually.

21: *Atlantis:* "On Cannibals" in Michel de Montaigne, *Essays,* trans. J. M. Cohen (New York: Penguin, 1958), p. 108.

23: Elizabeth Lapovsky Kennedy and Madeline D. Davis, *Boots of Leather, Slippers of Gold: The History of a Lesbian Community* (New York: Penguin, 1994).

24: Neal Ascherson, *Black Sea* (New York: Hill and Wang, 1995), pp. 4–5.

26: Eudora Welty, "Place in Fiction" in her *The Eye of the* Story (New York: Vintage, 1979), p. 118.

27: "Made in Buffalo," *Fortune,* July 1951, p. 91.

30: Reyner Banham, *A Concrete Atlantis: U.S. Industrial Building and European Modern Architecture* (Cambridge: MIT Press, 1989), pp. 19–20.

31: Gerrit Engel, *Buffalo Grain Elevators* (Berlin: n.p., 1997).

34: Margaret Atwood, *Cat's Eye* (New York: Bantam, 1989), p. 91.

36: Ibid., p. 371.

42: Gustave Flaubert, *Sentimental Education,* trans., Robert Baldick (New York: Penguin, 1986), p. 15.

43: *Annual ridership*: Norma Evenson, *Paris: A Century of Change, 1878–1978* (New Haven: Yale University Press, 1979), p. 90.

44: Charles Baudelaire, *The Painter of Modern Life and Other Essays*, trans. Jonathan Mayne (London: Phaidon, 1964); Walter Benjamin, "Paris, the Capital of the Nineteenth Century," in his *The Arcades Project*, trans. Howard Eiland and Kevin McLaughlin (Cambridge: Harvard University Press, 1999), pp. 3–26; Edmund White, *The Flâneur* (New York: Bloomsbury, 2001).

48: Marguerite Duras, *The War: A Memoir* (New York: Pantheon, 1986), pp. 10–15.

49: Laurence Sterne, *A Sentimental Journey through France and Italy* (New York: Penguin, 1967), p. 127.

54: *The Egyptian hieroglyph*: Fernand Braudel, *The Identity of France, Volume II: People and Population* (New York: HarperCollins, 1990), p. 426.

55: Honoré de Balzac, *The Wild Ass's Skin*, trans. Herbert J. Hunt (New York: Penguin, 1977), p. 29.

55: George Du Maurier, *Trilby* (New York: Harper and Brothers, 1894), p. 35.

57: Henry James, *The Ambassadors* (Boston: Houghton Mifflin, 1960), p. 335.

57: *Viking raiders*: Gwyn Jones, *A History of the Vikings*, rev. ed. (New York: Oxford University Press, 1984), pp. 224–25.

59: Roland Barthes, *The Eiffel Tower and Other Mythologies*, trans. Richard Howard (New York: Hill and Wang, 1979), p. 7.

60: Flaubert, *Sentimental Education*, p. 111.

61: Henri Murger, *La Bôheme: Scénes de la vie de Bòheme*, trans. Elizabeth Ward Hugus (Salt Lake City: Peregrine Smith, 1988; repr. of 1930 ed.), p. 82.

62: John Russell, *Paris* (New York: Abrams, 1983), p. 227.

64: Joseph Conrad, *Heart of Darkness and the Secret Sharer* (New York: Signet, n.d.), p. 67.

64: Jonathan Raban, *Soft City* (New York: Dutton, 1974), p. 105.

64: Walt Whitman, *Poetry and Prose*, ed. Justin Kaplan (New York: Library of America, 1982), pp. 308–9.

66: Montesquieu, *Persian Letters*, trans. C. J. Betts (New York: Penguin, 1973), p. 71.

66: Benjamin, "Paris, the Capital of the Nineteenth Century," pp. 3–26.

66: Fernand Braudel, *The Identity of France, Volume I: History and Environment* (New York: Harper and Row, 1988), p. 51.

67: Sterne, *Sentimental Journey*, p. 27.

67–68: Fanny Trollope: *Paris and the Parisians* (Gloucester and New York: Alan Sutton, 1985; rpr. of 1836 ed.), p. 498 (on Balzac), p. 56 (on Notre-Dame), and p. 214 (on Sterne).

68: Du Maurier, *Trilby*, p. 36.

68: Arthur Bartlett Maurice, *The Paris of the Novelists* (Garden City, NY: Doubleday, 1919), p. 124.

68: E. V. Lucas, *A Wanderer in Paris* (New York: Macmillan, 1913), p. 164.

69: Brassaï, *The Secret Paris of the Thirties*, trans. Richard Miller (New York: Pantheon, 1976), unpaginated.

74: Wallace Stevens, "A Mythology Reflects Its Region," *The Palm at the End of the Mind*, ed. Holly Stevens (New York: Vintage, 1972), p. 398.

75: *Exodusters*: James R. Green, *Grass-Roots Socialism: Radical Movements in the Southwest, 1895–1943* (Baton Rouge: Louisiana State University Press, 1978), p. 98.

75: N. Scott Momaday, *The Way to Rainy Mountain* (Albuquerque: University of New Mexico Press, 1985), p. 4.

76: Angie Debo, "History," in *The WPA Guide to 1930s Oklahoma*, ed. Anne Hodges Morgan (Lawrence: University Press of Kansas, 1989), p. 23.

77: Woody Guthrie, *Bound for Glory* (New York: Dutton, 1968; rpr. of 1943 ed.), p. 115.

78: Washington Irving, *A Tour on the Prairies*, ed. John Francis McDermott (Norman: University of Oklahoma Press, 1985), pp. 7, 10.

79: Ian Frazier, *Great Plains* (New York: Penguin, 1990), p. 12.

79: *Crossroads of America*: Governor Henry Bellmon, quoted in *The Saturday Oklahoman*, 7 October 1989, p. 1.

80: John Steinbeck, *The Grapes of Wrath*, introd. by Studs Terkel (New York: Viking, 1989), p. 160.

81: Edna Ferber, *Cimarron* (Garden City, NY: Doubleday, 1930), p. x.

84: *Debo submitted her manuscript. . .*: see Rennard Strickland, "Oklahoma's Story: Recording the History of the Forty-Sixth State," in *Oklahoma: New Views of the Forty-Sixth State*, ed. Anne Hodges Morgan and H. Wayne Morgan (Norman: University of Oklahoma Press, 1982), p. 238.

85: Lynn Riggs, *Green Grow the Lilacs: A Play* (New York: Samuel French, 1931), p. 157.

86: Frazier, *Great Plains*, p. 81.

90: Ferber, *Cimarron*, p. 186.

96: Momaday, *The Way to Rainy Mountain*, p. 5.

96: Alan Moorehead, *Cooper's Creek: The Opening of Australia* (New York: Atlantic Monthly Press, 1987; rpr. of 1963 ed.), p. 9.

98: Momaday, *The Way to Rainy Mountain*, p. 5.

101: Steinbeck, *The Grapes of Wrath*, p. 280.

102: Dan Morgan, *Rising in the West: The True Story of an "Okie" Family from the Great Depression through the Reagan Years* (New York: Knopf, 1992), p. 16.

102: Erskine Caldwell, *Around About America* (New York: Pocket Books, 1965), p. 99.

103: Mark Abley, *Beyond Forget: Rediscovering the Prairies* (Vancouver: Douglas and McIntyre, 1988), p. 197.

117: Gretel Ehrlich, *The Solace of Open Spaces* (New York: Penguin, 1985), p. 2.

120: John Brinckerhoff Jackson, *A Sense of Place, A Sense of Time* (New Haven: Yale University Press, 1994), p. viii.

122: Natasha Peterson, *Sacred Sites: A Traveler's Guide to North America's Most Powerful, Mystical Landmarks* (Chicago: Contemporary Books, 1988), p. 98.

124: Charles M. Doughty, *Travels in Arabia Deserta*, 2 vols., introd. by T. E. Lawrence (New York: Dover, 1979; rpr. of 3d ed. of 1936), Vol. 1, p. 487.

125: William Least Heat Moon, *Blue Highways: A Journey into America* (New York: Fawcett, 1984), p. xi.

130: Max Frisch, *Man in the Holocene* (New York: Harcourt Brace, 1980), p. 48.

130: Francis Parkman, *The Oregon Trail and the Conspiracy of Pontiac*, ed. William R. Taylor (New York: Library of America, 1991), p. 63.

134: Henry Beston, *The Outermost House: A Year of Life on the Great Beach of Cape Cod* (New York: Viking, 1970), p. 156.

136: *By the reckoning of archaeologists. . .*: See Graham and Anna Ritchie, *Scotland: Archaeology and Early History* (Edinburgh: Edinburgh University Press, 1991).

137: Edwin Muir, *An Autobiography* (London: Hogarth Press, 1954), p. 206.

138: Emily Hiestand, *The Very Rich Hours: Travels in Orkney, Belize, the Everglades, and Greece* (Boston: Beacon Press, 1992), pp. 180–81.

143: Christa Wolf, "Unter den Linden," in her *What Remains and Other Stories*, trans. Heike Schwarzbauer and Rick Takvorian (Chicago: University of Chicago Press, 1995), p. 77.

147: Brian Ladd, *The Ghosts of Berlin: Confronting German History in the Urban Landscape* (Chicago: University of Chicago Press, 1997).

189: Albert Camus, *Notebooks: 1942–51*, trans. Justin O'Brien (New York: Harcourt Brace, 1978), p. 78.